The Wisdom of Wolves

The Wisdom of Wolves

How they think, plan and look after each other – amazing
facts about the animal that is more like man than any other

ELLI H. RADINGER

Translated by Shaun Whiteside

MICHAEL JOSEPH
an imprint of
PENGUIN BOOKS

MICHAEL JOSEPH

UK | USA | Canada | Ireland | Australia
India | New Zealand | South Africa

Michael Joseph is part of the Penguin Random House group of companies
whose addresses can be found at global.penguinrandomhouse.com

First published in Germany by Ludwig Verlag 2017
Published in the United Kingdom by Michael Joseph 2019
001

Copyright © Ludwig Verlag, a division of Random House Germany, 2017
Translation copyright © Shaun Whiteside, 2019

The moral right of the author has been asserted

We assume no liability for the content of any third-party websites listed in this publication
and do not adopt them as our own, but merely refer to them at the time of the first publication.

Set in 12/14.75 pt Bembo Book MT Std
Typeset by Jouve (UK), Milton Keynes
Printed and bound in Great Britain by Clays Ltd, Elcograf S.p.A.

A CIP catalogue record for this book is available from the British Library

HARDBACK ISBN: 978–0–241–34671–6
OM PAPERBACK ISBN: 978–0–241–34672–3

www.greenpenguin.co.uk

For Andrea – alias 'Schnösel'

Contents

Introduction: How I Kissed a Wolf and Became Addicted   1

The Importance of Family: Why It's Important to
Look After Those Entrusted to Us   11

Leadership on the Alpha Principle: You Don't Always
Have to be the Boss   33

The Strength of Women: What Connects Women
and Wolves   47

The Wisdom of Old Age: Why We Can't Do Without
the Elderly   59

The Art of Communication: How a Shared Song Can
Establish Trust   67

The Longing for Home: Why We Need a Place Where
We Belong   77

I'm Off Then: On Going Away and Arriving   89

Almost Best Friends: How in Spite of All Your
Differences You Can be a Perfect Team   101

Planning for Success – the Wolf Method: Why It's
Important to Have a Plan   113

The Right Moment: Why Waiting Sometimes
Brings Us Forward   131

The Game of Life: Why We Should Never Stop Playing   139

When Bad Things Happen to Good Wolves:
  Overcoming Fears of Loss and Surviving Bad Times   149

Let's Just Save the World: The Secret of an Intact
  Ecosystem   163

Wolf Medicine: How the Magic of Wolves Can Heal Us   173

Of Men and Wolves: A Difficult Relationship Between
  Love and Hate   189

Welcome Wolf: Living with Wolves in Germany   203

Epilogue: WWWD   219

Appendix: Tips for Wolf Tours in Yellowstone
  and Germany   225

Thanks   237

Sources   239

Picture Credits   244

Introduction

How I Kissed a Wolf and Became Addicted

There's a first time for everything. For my special relationship with wolves there were three 'first times': the first wolf kiss, the first wild wolf and the first German wolf.

I had my first wolf kiss from Imbo, a six-year-old male timber wolf in an American wolf sanctuary. I had left behind my old life as an attorney-at-law in Frankfurt, Germany. Crimes, rent disputes and divorces were increasingly frustrating me. Instead of helping justice to victory with great vigour, I was coming to dread every legal meeting. I lacked the detachment and the abrasiveness to be a good lawyer. I wanted to fulfil my life's dream, and combine my love of writing with the fascination I had for wolves.

Without any biological background, but with a great deal of passion and optimism, I applied for an ethology internship at Wolf Park, a wolf research institute in Indiana. At the preliminary interview the director of research, Dr Erich Klinghammer, explained that the alpha wolf of the main pack alone decides whether the trainee will be appointed.

But how do you apply to a wolf? Luckily I didn't need to dance or sing or perform any other tricks, but I swear I couldn't have been more excited if I'd been applying for *The X Factor* – although that was precisely the wrong emotion to show when meeting a captive wolf, Klinghammer said. 'You have to stay completely cool! He'll sense your excitement.'

You try staying cool when you're facing a 50-kilo furry packet of muscles that's staring at you with yellow eyes. At that moment I thought of my German shepherd, friend and confidant of my childhood. Fine. Basically Imbo was just a big dog – a very big dog. Two pages of safety instructions had prepared me for the meeting, and provided legal insurance for the director of the sanctuary. I signed a waiver with the frightening wording: *I understand that there is a risk of injury, and that the injuries can be serious.*

Armed with this warning, I entered the wolf enclosure with two keepers, tried to stand firm and took a deep breath. Then my world was reduced to the wolf that approached me at an elegant trot. The silver stripes of his coat gleamed in the afternoon sunlight. His black nose sniffed my scent deeply, his ears pointing alertly forward. From the corners of my eyes I saw the other members of Imbo's pack waiting by the fence. They were clearly tense as they waited to see if I would pass the test and the boss would accept me. So was I, because it was only then that I would be able to start my internship. Right now the most important thing was to survive the next few seconds.

The film in my head slowed right down. The wolf's powerful hindquarters lowered slightly as he prepared to jump. As he flew towards me and I pressed against him with all my strength, there was no turning back. His paws, the size of side plates, landed on my shoulders, and his imposing fangs were only a centimetre from my face. The world stopped. Then he licked my face with his rough tongue. That 'kiss' was my introduction to the 'drug' wolf.

After Imbo had accepted me, my internship with the wolves of Wolf Park began. I learned everything about the attitude and behaviour of captive wolves, I hand-raised wolf pups with a bottle and over the following months enjoyed countless wet kisses from Imbo and the rest of the pack.

Half a year later, when I moved to the wilderness of Minnesota, I had received an excellent training and thought I knew everything about wolves. Then I met my first wild wolf.

The log cabin in which I lived was far from civilization near a lake in the middle of wolf and bear territory. Early on New Year's Day I pulled on my snowshoes in minus 30 degrees Celsius to go off in search of wolf tracks. So far I hadn't had a glimpse of my grey neighbours; only their howls told me that they were there. But the previous night, when I stood for a long time outside the cabin, listening to the chorus of wolves, gazing fascinated at the polar lights, a movement on the lake had distracted me from the celestial spectacle. Four wolves had run across the shimmering surface of the ice and were chasing something before they disappeared over the horizon. I couldn't make out what they were pursuing.

I set off the next morning to try to find them. I carefully followed their tracks into the forest. They led into the dense woodland, over sticks and stones, through bushes, past cliffs and boulders and across vast snow-covered surfaces. I sometimes came across a circular depression, presumably the resting spot of a deer. Abundant yellow markings in the snow showed that the wolves had discovered the same place as well. After an hour of tracking I found fresh traces of blood and a short time later found a dead young white-tailed deer. I knelt down and touched it. Its belly had been torn open and one back leg was missing. The stomach lay off to the side, the heart and liver were gone. Bite wounds on the throat and legs indicated that the animal hadn't suffered for long.

There was no sign of the wolves anywhere, but suddenly I felt as if I was being watched. I was still kneeling in the snow. Not a good position if a hungry wolf is standing behind you. I got to my feet in slow motion and turned round. There he stood, only a few metres away. A grey wolf. The hairs on the back of his neck bristling as if he had walked through an electric field, his ears pricked, he tilted his head slightly to one side and watched me closely. His nostrils vibrated as he tried to pick up my scent, but the wind was coming from the other direction. I could tell by looking at him that this young animal had no idea who or what I was. I held my breath. Of course wild wolves don't attack humans, but did this wolf know that? He was hungry, and I was standing between him and the food he had fought hard for.

'Hi, wolf!' Was that my voice croaking?

The animal flinched and jumped back. At the same time he tucked his half-raised tail under his belly. Curiosity had turned to fear. He turned a half-pirouette on his hindquarters and shot into the forest. Fascinated, I stared for a long time at the trees he had disappeared behind.

Over the following months with the biologists of the International Wolf Center in Ely in the north of Minnesota, and with the wolves outside my cabin, I learned more about the life and behaviour of wolves in the wild, about research, telemetry and monitoring.

In 1995, when the first Canadian timber wolves were established in Yellowstone National Park, the next wolfish part of my life began. I worked as a volunteer on the Yellowstone Wolf Project and assisted the biologists with their field research. I stayed mostly in the Lamar Valley in the north of the national park, known as the 'Serengeti of America' because of the diversity of its species. This is where the big herds of elk* and bison gather in

---

* In North America the European red deer is called an 'elk' or a 'wapiti'. It is larger than the European red deer, has longer antlers and is more adapted to the cold climate. Male and female elk have neck manes, while only the male European red deer have manes. In North America the European 'elk' is also called a 'moose'.

winter. It's the land of milk and honey for predators. Here at an altitude of 2,500 metres I was observing the wolf families that lived there and reporting my observations to the biologists.

That was over twenty years ago. Since then I've had more than 10,000 wolf sightings. Sometimes we were only a few metres apart. I've never felt threatened or scared. For me it was a great privilege to see the animals almost every day. To experience that, I flew 10,000 kilometres across the Atlantic several times a year because, officially, Germany had no wolves. When these timid animals were confirmed here in the year 2000, I never dared to hope I would ever get to see one.

It was another ten years before I saw a wolf in the wild for the first time in Germany. I was coming back from a reading, taking the express train from Leipzig to Frankfurt. The attendant set a cappuccino down on my table, and I was about to pick up a newspaper when I looked out of the window and spotted something brown in a field. When you spend a long time in nature with animals, you develop an ability not unlike the visual imprinting that wolves have of prey or a landscape in their heads. Unconsciously I absorb a scene that I see, and sense that something's not quite right, even before I can define it in concrete terms. That feeling stirred in me now all of a sudden. What was that? Legs too long for a fox. Long tail, so not a deer. *Stop the train*, I thought. But it dashed relentlessly on. I pressed my face to the glass, leaned over the table and tipped my cappuccino over my paper. Yes, a wolf! It was standing still, staring at something on the edge of the forest. Then the picture dissolved again with the speed of the train. That was the first and, so far, the only time that I was lucky enough to see a wild wolf in Germany.

Observing wolves in the wilderness is an endless story. You are there when they mate; a few months later you see the result fumbling out of the den on little short legs; you watch them fighting for the best place at Mum's 'milk bar'; you rejoice at their first hesitant attempts at hunting (hurray – a mouse!); you suffer with them when they hurt themselves; you mourn their deaths, laugh at their fun and games, follow their attempts at flirting – until the cycle closes again and it all starts over from the beginning.

I am a self-confessed 'wolfaholic', and I suffer from withdrawal symptoms when I'm not with them. For many people it's enough if they see a wolf once or twice in their lives. Not me. I want more from them. So I wait until the next wolf sighting – whether it's at minus 40 degrees, or in scorching sunshine surrounded by stinging flies. I put on a few extra socks, put little heating pads in my gloves or cover myself with sun cream and mosquito spray. And then I stand there for hours unwaveringly, regardless of the weather. I do that because I know that wolves do things that I don't want to miss. And if they happen not to be doing something, I want to know what they're going to do next.

If there are no wolves there, I wait till they come. And if they suddenly do appear, I feel that something special is happening. They are intense moments, when the world feels vivid and very consistent.

I feel blessed that wolves let me take part in their lives – by watching their hunting, mating and the raising of their young. I've discovered that they are very similar to human beings in their behaviour: they are loving family members, firm but fair leaders, sympathetic helpers, crazed teenagers or silly jokers. My observations have taught me that the wolf is a great teacher from whom we can learn a lot about life.

Wolf packs have become a part of my life. Studying their complex social behaviour for so long has changed me. Concepts such as morality, responsibility and love have acquired a new meaning for me. The wolves are my teachers and the source of my inspiration. Every day they teach me to see the world with other eyes – theirs.

The Importance of Family

Why It's Important to Look After Those Entrusted to Us

The wolves lay rolled up in the snow for a long time. They looked like a circle of grey stones, and sometimes an ear or a paw could be seen twitching. A slender female wolf stretched out and lay down on her side. A silver stripe ran along her underbelly and through her dark grey coat. The others had dark fur on their backs, with rust-coloured patches on their chests. The wolf parents rested a few metres away, their backs pressed against each other, the two-year-old wolves and yearlings distributed around them, exhausted by chasing and tugging games with their brothers and sisters.

The little ones were just waking up. They jostled one another and jumped on the ones who were still asleep. For a few minutes they looked like a gang of over-excited teenagers. Then they shook themselves and looked around. A yearling was the first to pull away and jumped over the dozing adults, with the others following him. The youngest slipped out and skidded into his father, who jumped up and growled at him. Immediately, Junior rolled on to his back and whimpered, and his father licked his face. Now the little rascals came back. They jumped at the leader, rolled in the snow with him and dashed away. That woke up the other adult family members.

The young wolves ran over to their parents and covered them with kisses, licks and small affectionate bites. They jumped over them and jostled them, forming a huge knot of wolves, so that it was hard to say where one began and the next ended. They lovingly enclosed their siblings' muzzles in their teeth, they twisted and rubbed and touched each other, crawled under tree trunks, hopped over cliffs and dived among bushes that blocked their path. There were flashing eyes and wagging propeller tails everywhere. The most eager leapt into the thick of it, just to be there. An expression of the pure joy of life.

One of them climbed on to a hill, followed by his younger brothers. They looked at each other, then skidded over the edge and down the snow covered slope. As they did, they spun on their own axis and left a cloud of snowy dust. By the time they reached the bottom they looked like Arctic wolves.

At last one of the group raised his voice. Others joined in. Then almost all of them stood up and howled in their different pitches. Some sang, others yelped with excitement; two wolves lying down raised their heads and howled along. The song rose into the air in a crescendo and exploded in a magnificent finale.

The first wolves ran off. A few young wolves were still playing catch. But then the whole family started moving and marched in single file over the mountain crest.

Few scenes in nature are as heart-warming to observe as a wolf family. In contrast to the growling, fang-flashing creatures that we see in films, the life of wild wolves is characterized by harmony as well as by playful and affectionate interactions. The pups are the beloved and protected treasures of the pack* and are treated accordingly. Not only the parents but the whole family looks after them, including aunts, uncles and older brothers and sisters, in a way that can only be described as altruistic, or self-less. Old and wounded family members are brought food and never abandoned. Every member of the pack knows where their place is, and who decides. They all confirm their affection and attention to one another through constant interactions and rit-uals. In the wild strong family bonds are important for protection and survival.

The social system of wolf packs is the focus of many studies both by biologists and psychologists, who agree that man can learn a lot about himself by watching wolves. To gain a better understanding of their social behaviour, biological behavi-ourists have classified wolves into two different fundamental character types:

Type A is the risk-taking, assertive and extroverted type. They are determined to have their own way and in situations that are new to them, and which they cannot control by their behaviour, they are quickly overstrained. After a failure they need long pauses. Such wolfish (and human) personalities are normally cheerful, but also exhausting – at least as long as they can sort things out on their own terms. If they can't, they become confused and call for help.

Type B is quite different. Their main attitude to life is one of distinguished reservation. Introverted characters prefer to first

---

* A wolf pack usually consists of a pair of parents and their descendants (the offspring of the first and the next generation), as well as individual uncles and aunts. So they are a family in the biological sense. Sometimes it may also hap-pen that foreign wolves are accepted into the pack. In modern wolf research (field research) the terms 'pack' and 'wolf family' are used to mean the same thing. A pack is a wolf family and vice versa.

wait and see what happens next, but are more successful in adapting.

A wolf family consists fundamentally of a collection of these personality types. The two leaders, the parents, almost always consist of a combination of types A and B, which complement one another. But that does not mean that type A is always the male and type B always the female.

These different character types also exist among human beings. Have you already asked yourself which one you belong to? If you are the extrovert A-type, you have to learn to control yourself in certain situations, and to not be too impulsive in your actions. As a cautious, shy B-type, you sometimes have the problem of acting too slowly, not reacting quickly enough. Think of the saying 'The early bird catches the worm'.

Of course there are all kinds of variations of these two personality types. I see myself as a milder form of the B-type with slight hints of A.

This insight has also helped me with human relationships, for example: he's just A or B and can't help it. Critics of the A-B classification point out that even fundamental characters can change at any time. But my own experience is that our underlying personality always comes back to the surface in the end, in spite of efforts to the contrary. As they say, 'A leopard can't change its spots'.

Like individual wolves, wolf families have a kind of group personality. For example, many packs are characterized by autocratic rulers or aggravating individuals. These individual characters make one pack fundamentally friendlier, like the Druid wolves,† and another more feared, like the Mollie wolves.

---

† The wolf packs in Yellowstone generally take their names from the areas where they have their territory. The Druid wolves, for example, lived at the foot of Druid Peak. Exceptions to this are the Leopold pack, named after the

A Druid yearling (A-type) nonchalantly crosses
the road, ignoring the cars

The Lamar wolves in Yellowstone, on the other hand, demonstrate both personality types. That becomes particularly clear
when they cross a road with tourists and cars on it. The A-types
do this confidently and independently; they don't hesitate and
cross the road straight away, sometimes without even looking at
the people. The B-types, however, are willing to cross the road
in only an extreme emergency. I remember when in May 2011 a
very cautious adult B-wolf was trying to cross the road, but
didn't dare to because of all the tourists. He wanted to wait for

environmentalist Aldo Leopold, and the Mollie pack. The Mollies were
named, because of their power and strength, after Mollie Beattie, the main
advocate of wolf reintroduction, who died of cancer shortly after the return
of the wolves.

darkness, and was looking for a hiding place. But that brought him too close to a coyote den. The coyote parents came flying out and attacked him. Already irritated by the tourists and now also chased by his small relatives' screaming maddening yelps, and biting him on the backside, he took to his heels and ran to the road, right through the group of people. Presumably that was the lesser evil for him.

Since 2012, wolves in the USA have been taken off the Endangered Species List, and can now be hunted even on the edges of Yellowstone. In the national park they are still protected. But wolves don't stick to borders. They stray from the park and then face the rifles of the hunters. I wonder whether in situations like that B-types, like the scared wolf mentioned above, have better chances of survival. The brave ones may conquer the world, but the quiet, timid ones survive.

Among mammals, power structures are already established by family order. Parents decide for children, older siblings for younger ones. This means that a ranking must not be fought out through battles or politics or – as dog owners will know – who is allowed on the sofa and who isn't. Parents don't need to prove that they are in charge. They are. On the basis of their experience they determine the well-being and safety of the group, because they want the best for all.

Among wolves, everything revolves around the family. It is their foundation, safety, stability, the point of their entire existence. For the family they are even prepared to sacrifice their life. In April 2013 I was standing with other wolf-watchers on a hill in the Lamar Valley to catch a glimpse of the area where the Lamar wolves had their den. It was five days since the birth of the pack's pups. Suddenly I saw sixteen wolves from the Mollie pack running into the den forest. I feared the worst. Then seventeen wolves came back out of the forest, with the Lamar alpha female in front. She was running for her life. A few days previously she had given birth to four pups and was weakened. The Mollies were quickly catching up and I held my breath. She ran up to a steep cliff. Soon she would have to stop and face her pursuers, who could easily kill her. Her helpless pups would die too. Either the Mollies would kill them in the den or they would starve to death.

But we had underestimated the wolf's will to live. She ran to the road where the tourists were standing. As she was used to people, she crossed the road, stopped and looked back at the Mollies, who didn't dare to follow.

Even though the alpha wolf was now safe, her family was still in danger. Standing between her and her young were her attackers, who only needed to turn round and go back to the den to kill the puppies.

At that moment a two-year-old daughter of hers appeared right beside the Mollies, who immediately attacked her. The daughter ran eastwards, away from the den, with the Mollies following close behind. This young wolf was one of the fastest in the pack and knew every stone and shrub in their territory. She was easily able to escape the attack.

The Mollies ran crossly back and forth a few times, and then headed back to their territory. That year they didn't reappear in the Lamar Valley. As soon as the attackers were gone, the alpha female ran back to her pups. A few weeks later I saw her with her offspring, all healthy and cheerful.

Family – it changes everything. For our family we're willing to sacrifice.

Even though it has often been written off, the family is not on the way out – it still carries on. The term 'family' does not apply only to traditional marriage, but also to 'patchwork' families, solo parents and same-sex partnerships.

The more fast-paced and complex the outside world, the more we yearn for family and old values, such as community, honesty, trust and loyalty. In the face of a challenging reality that makes too many demands on us, we flee into a clearly defined and reliable world. The morals of the wild late 1960s, when we rebelled against the establishment with its traditional role models, have made way for those of the 1950s. Suddenly we are happy once again with our old-fashioned furniture and our allotments, and have no problem being seen as boring and bourgeois.

Wolves are bourgeois par excellence. They love the values we yearn for. With numerous rituals they communicate to each other constancy and dependability.

Rituals are a significant component of the life of a wolf family, and contribute to the stability of their relationships: the waking ceremony that I described at the start of the chapter, the greeting of the parents when they come home after a hunting expedition, the group howling.

Family rituals are indispensable for humans too. They bring closeness, community and orientation, and strengthen solidarity. We notice their importance in daily life only when they disappear.

The kind of rituals we used to have – going to church on Sunday, followed by lunch round the table and a visit to Granny – barely occur in modern families. If we can get the whole family together for a meal once a day, that's already valuable.

In my hectic everyday life, I try to keep one day a week free for my family or friends. Our shared experience encourages the feeling of belonging and reinforces the individual's sense of identity, and thus their basic trust in not being abandoned. At the same time it's important to maintain family rituals consistently. As a rule, children are keen on such rituals because that kind of fixed routine structures their everyday life, and a regular meal together is an opportunity to reinforce communication between parents and children.

Young wolves need to learn for life as well. They do that by observing their parents and imitating them. Even though little wolves seem to have freedom to do whatever they want to, their parents sometimes need to set boundaries.

Early one summer I observed a family of wolves moving through the Lamar Valley in Yellowstone. One young wolf dawdled along behind. There was always something more exciting to discover and sniff at than staying with the pack. His family waited for him a few times until he caught up. But eventually they had had enough. The wolves ran on and left the dreamer behind. When he realized that he was lost, he panicked and started howling long and loud to call them back. That had always worked in the past, but not this time. It wasn't until the evening that the wolf family came to collect the visibly relieved youngster. He had learned his lesson, and from then on he stayed with the group.

That is how education works according to the wolf method: nothing is forbidden to the young wolf – he can have his own experiences and learns that actions have consequences. Wolf parents teach their offspring by treading a carefully judged line between good-natured bonhomie and strictness, social togetherness and boundary setting.

In one respect the wolves' method of child-rearing differs from that of many human parents: they are united, and present a solid front. The little wolves have no chance of playing their parents off against each other along the lines of: 'If Dad doesn't let me do that, Mum will.' In matters of rearing, the whole wolf family sticks together, uncles and aunts included. They are all involved in disciplining the offspring. And so the adult wolves also stay out of it when a yearling disciplines a pup who is getting on his nerves too much.

Wolf pups, like human children, need parents to show them the way. They are role models from whom they can learn and who – if necessary – also set boundaries.

A wolf mother disciplines her annoying puppy with
a bite over the muzzle

In the rearing of young, the whole family is concerned with
the younger generation. While the pups are still being suckled
in the den, the father and the older siblings bring food for the
mother. Later all the family members look after the offspring by
regurgitating predigested food for them.

Wolf fathers are absolutely crazy about their pups. The
powerful leading wolf of the Druid pack was also an enthusiastic father. Not only did he lovingly look after his own
offspring, he even adopted some of his grandchildren after one
of his daughters had returned pregnant to the bosom of the family after a brief tête-à-tête with an alien wolf. One of the
favourite activities of the leading wolf was playing and wrest-
ling with pups. The thing he liked best of all was to pretend to
be losing. He would let one of the little wolves jump at him and
bite his fur. Then he threw himself on his back, while the little
one stood on top of him, tail wagging.

The ability to pretend – in this case pretending to be defeated – shows that the animal understands how their behaviour is perceived by others. It is a sign of intelligence. And the little ones definitely knew that the 'submission' was only a piece of play-acting, but in that way they were able to experience what it feels like to conquer something much larger than themselves. Wolves need that kind of confidence every day of their lives.

But wolf parents aren't perfect either. They too can sometimes be moody; they show irritation, frustration, rage and impatience, just like when us humans get out of bed on the wrong side in the morning. But they can also show joy, love, enthusiasm and a sense of fun. These emotions change often, as with human beings. But if wolf parents behave impatiently in certain situations, that changes nothing about the fundamentally trusting relationships between the family members.

Even the yearlings in a wolf family take loving care of their younger siblings. Their role is irreplaceable and helps the family to survive. If a litter fails to survive one year, the help of these absent siblings will be missed the following year when rearing the pups.

I was able to experience a special moment of love among siblings one spring, when the melting snow had transformed the rivers into raging torrents. This is the time when a wolf family moves from the den into the hunting ground, the so-called rendezvous territory. To do that they sometimes have to cross rivers. The adults swim ahead and show the little ones how it's done. They howl from the opposite shore and encourage them to follow. I saw one pup who didn't dare to go in, and ran up and down wailing on the bank. Again and again he dipped a paw in the water and turned round despondently. In the end his sister swam back, grabbed a stick lying on the shore and distracted the pup with pulling games. Then she enticed him into the water with the stick and helped him to the other side.

In a wolf family every member is important to the group and has a place where they are needed. That place is not determined by the parents or the leading wolves. Instead, the young wolves find out their strengths early on, and jump in of their own accord when needed. There are swift instigators who are indispensable when hunting, in deep snow the strongest run ahead and leave a trail, while particularly patient wolves are excellent babysitters.

We humans also have individual abilities that we can deploy for the good of the family or in our work. Some of us are patient and good listeners, others are impulsive and take new ideas further. Yet others are peacemakers and skilled negotiators. So in every pack there are personalities that are able to re-establish peace. They position themselves between the snapping, growling brawlers and wait, stoical, relaxed and aware of their inner strength. When the waves have stilled and everyone has calmed down, the wolves resume their daily business.

As so often when I observe the family lives of wolves, I wonder why everything seems to be so much more complicated for us bipeds. Is it because the family isn't at the heart of our lives, as it is for wolves?

No! Quite the contrary. In the present day the family is stronger than ever, and relationships between parents and children unlike anything else in history. That was the result of the Shell Youth Study in 2015. Almost 90 per cent of all young people have a good relationship with their parents, and almost three quarters would like to bring up their children as they themselves were brought up. They hold the view that one needs a family in order to have a happy life. At a time when the demands of school, training and the first years of work are rising, most young people find backing and emotional support in their parents. However, even if we wish to see the family at the centre of our lives, for humans – unlike wolves – there are sometimes gulfs between wishful thinking and everyday reality.

In a wolf pack all members take their bearings from the experienced leaders, who, as parents, exert responsibility and decide what is best for the family. Of course each individual wolf also has the possibility to go its own way or protest against the decisions made by the leaders. They are at liberty to do that. However, the experienced leaders still enjoy the greatest respect. A wolf family functions thanks to its close and unconditional solidarity and mutual care. Sometimes you read about old or sick wolves being killed by the pack. That may happen in an unnatural enclosure situation, but it doesn't apply to reality in the wild. I have often experienced situations when wolves have been wounded during hunts or in fights with competitors. Their families have always looked after them. If they went hunting, one of them would stay with the one who has been injured. When they came back, the hunters would bring food with them. I once even saw wolves regurgitating meat for an old wolf, something normally done only for pups. Sick and old animals are fed until they recover.

It is precisely in this quality of care that humans and wolves are very similar. Even with the great apes, adult male animals only care for the offspring as long as they are very young. Bringing in food all year and looking after the other family members when they are ill are qualities that we find in both sexes only in humans and wolves.

Chimpanzees might at first sight seem more similar to humans than wolves. But male primates don't help to feed the young or look after the old. Wolves and humans understand one another better. That is one of the reasons why a long time ago we invited not monkeys but wolves to share our lives. Wolves, dogs and humans – no wonder we found each other. We were made for one another.

Both birth and social conditions decide who belongs to the wolf family. If, for example, an unusually large number of animals in a pack are related to each other, it is easier for outsiders to be accepted. In that way wolves avoid incest, and genetic diversity is maintained.

I saw a stranger being accepted into a family one sunny winter day in 2003 in Yellowstone. The Druid pack, a group of seven animals, had assumed the dominant role in the valley. The alpha wolf, number 21‡, was like the leading man in a movie. The next time I saw him, I was struck by his powerful build: a wide ribcage, stout legs, dark grey fur with a dark strip from forehead to nose and an unusually short bushy tail. You could recognize him at first sight. When he appeared, the wolf world seemed to hold his breath. He radiated natural authority. His partner looked similar, the way old couples often resemble one another. She had the same marking on her face, but she was more delicate and a bit paler on the shoulders. The Druids were the undisputed rulers of their hunting ground and regularly patrolled its borders. One day a strange wolf approached the pack.

It was Super Bowl Sunday, the first Sunday in February, and one of the biggest sporting events in America. The football fans stayed at home in front of their TVs, which meant that for a change the park was almost deserted. The breeding season had begun – always the highlight of the wolf year for me. About thirty centimetres of snow had fallen in the night, and I had to wait until the snowplough had cleared the road from my cabin in Silver Gate to the entrance of the park. I made some sandwiches, filled a Thermos with hot coffee, packed everything in my rucksack and set off for Lamar Valley. I drove slowly along the road, stopped in every lay-by and scoured the valley for wolves with my binoculars. As so often, I didn't have to wait for long. Minus 24 degrees Celsius, and bright sunshine, that

‡ In Yellowstone researchers give the wolves not names but numbers. They are the numbers on their collars.

was the backdrop against which the stars of Lamar Valley made their appearance. Near the Soda Butte, an extinct geyser, I saw a few dark dots. The Druids were on the move. They looked full and well rested, and were bursting with *joie de vivre*. After they had frolicked exuberantly for a while on the slopes of the north side of the valley, they lay down to rest on the crest of the mountains.

Suddenly and unexpectedly the scene changed. A single wolf appeared in the valley and ran purposefully towards the wolf pack, which had its full complement of seven animals. So the adventurer could only have been a stranger. I hoped he would turn round quickly, because in the hunting ground of another pack he was in dangerous territory.

By now the Druids had spotted him as well. Heads raised and ears pricked, they lay tensely crowded together and focused their attention completely on the newcomer. The alpha pair stood on a hill as if made of stone and looked down at him. He went on marching into enemy territory unconcerned. I wasn't sure whether he hadn't yet discovered the Druids, or whether he was behaving so brazenly on purpose.

Excited, I went and got my spotting scope from the car, set it up and got myself in position. This powerful telescope is an indispensable tool and helps me identify the wolves.

The interloper was attractive and stately, with shiny pitch-black fur and gold-coloured eyes. All the females must have gone weak at the knees just at the sight of him.

And sure enough – I saw a slight movement in the Druid pack: a single tail-tip began twitching and cautiously wagging. Apparently I wasn't the only one who had been struck by the wolf's beauty.

By now he was approaching more slowly, his gait stiffer and more deliberate. His courage seemed to be giving way to reason. He stalked still further, and had almost reached the foot

Casanova, the Druids' heart-throb

of the mountain on which the Druids were now all standing in a row.

But the stranger wasn't about to give up. He ventured further towards the pack – this time with a deliberate look at the female wolf who had courageously extended the movement of the tip of her tail to the rest of it. I saw Cupid's arrow whirring through the air between the two wolves. I had forgotten the cold long ago, and I went on watching the ancient theatre of nature, holding my breath.

The brown wolf with the wagging tail became cheekier. She stood up and looked down at her suitor from the mountain slope like Juliet looking at Romeo from her balcony. That was too much for her father. He made himself even bigger than he already was and charged at the interloper. A short scuffle, a small bite, and the bold black wolf, whom I had christened Casanova, fled – but only a few metres. Then he turned round and, with his tail held lightly between his legs, tried to make it up to the boss. At last he lay down in the snow, while the leader climbed back to his vantage point.

Meanwhile Juliet, the brown wolf, had crawled down the slope a little way on her belly and was approaching the black wolf, who leapt up and, with a violent wag of his tail, dancing around and demanding to play, unleashed all his charm on her. The pair ran together side by side, jostled in mid-air and looked like a unit.

The parents seemed also to have succumbed to the attraction of the new arrival. After a few half-hearted efforts to chase him away, they gave up.

Casanova cautiously tried to entice the Druid daughter away from the pack. He managed to do so to a certain distance. The young wolf clearly felt torn between her potential new partner and her family. When the pack got up and moved on, she didn't know what to do. She kept running back and forth between the heartbreaker and her family. But family ties were stronger for the female than her desire to follow the potential lover. At last she opted for the safety of the pack and stayed with her parents.

The thwarted roué changed tactics. Hesitantly approaching with social gestures of submissiveness, he asked the father of his intended to accept him into the wolf family. He crept carefully behind the pack, but when Dad wasn't looking he rose into a proud posture and flirted with Juliet. Whenever the alpha male ran at him he threw himself on his back with his tail between his legs and waited until the leader had made his position clear. The alpha female stayed out of it all. She watched the drama, and her little daughter kept coming back to her mother between her escapades, trying to reassure her by licking the corners of her mouth.

Casanova's tactic was clearly successful, because when the

Druids disappeared over the mountain at the end of the day he was in the middle of them.

I had watched a strange wolf being accepted into another family. There had been no fight to drive the rival away. The pack leader had showed his authority by briefly beating up the intruder a number of times and driving him a little way off. That was enough to make his position obvious. Wolves are very well aware that it takes more strength and energy to fight something to the last than the supposed gain is worth.

The pack leader could afford to accept a stranger into his family. An underlying friendly and harmonic atmosphere in the group contributes more to a sense of solidarity than any arguments.

Casanova had demonstrated a high degree of social intelligence by behaving skilfully. He had entered strange territory in search of a partner, and exposed himself to the risk of infuriating the pack and being killed as a competitor. He had reacted correctly by alternating between attraction and fear when the pack leader ran at him. He had wedged his tail between his legs and fled just far enough away to make it known to the leader that he was not a threat. Later he immediately rolled on his back when the boss approached, and licked his face. If he had behaved otherwise, it could have meant the end.

How does a wolf family form in the first place? Very traditionally at first, just as humans do: boy meets girl, they have children and become a family. But as we have already seen, anything is possible among wolves. Whether they form a social group depends on their individual personalities, but also on chance encounters. Sometimes two or three brothers of a family migrate and find a family of their own. Very similar to what humans do. And as with humans, among wolves there are individuals who follow rules, those who break them and those who have their own variation of family life.

The success story of many famous wolf packs in Yellowstone extends over several generations. What's their secret?

For a group to succeed, all members must work together and be led by confident personalities. This applies to wolf packs as much as it does to large human families and dynasties. The successful ones always place the interests of the community above those of the individual. That ensures long-term survival.

Every wolf family's recipe for success is based on three principles: firstly concentration on the essential, which means everyone working together for the good of the family; secondly, constant communication and shared rituals; and, thirdly, strong leadership.

Leadership on the Alpha Principle

You Don't Always Have to be the Boss

It's early in the morning. Twelve wolves are drifting through the valley. The alpha wolves are ahead of everyone else. The rest of the pack follows, and right at the back, tail between his legs, is the omega wolf. He keeps his distance and doesn't dare advance any further because he would be bitten by the alphas and reminded of his lowly rank.

What's wrong with this image? Everything! I've made it up. Instead, what I saw that morning in Lamar Valley in Yellowstone was the following: twelve wolves drifted through the valley, at their head the powerful one- and two-year-old males. They ploughed a path through the deep snow, saving the male and female pack leaders energy. Further behind, some of the young females strolled along as if on a shopping spree. Last of all, some distance behind, the little ones dawdled, sniffing at some exciting spot or annoying a few ravens. Suddenly they all stopped dead as if obeying an order, and all looked in the same direction. I followed their gaze, but couldn't see anything. Clearly the wolves had discovered a possible danger. The last young wolf had now worked out what was going on, after violently colliding with his already stationary brother. There was a distinct sense of tension. Now the other wolves stepped aside and looked around for the alphas, who moved to the front and took the lead without hesitating. The group lined up behind them. Even the little ones were attentive now, and no longer easily distracted.

What I was seeing was a demonstration of exemplary leadership behaviour. No domination, no reprimands, no aggression, just silent authority and the assumption of responsibility.

So why is the first picture, the one I made up, evoked when people describe a wolf pack?

'Leading Like an Alpha' or 'Alpha Leadership' is very much the fashion. For a lot of money, the participants in management seminars spend a weekend learning 'wolfish leadership behaviour'. They all sit down in a wolf enclosure and watch how the alpha wolf dominates his pack. Ridiculous and absurd, in fact, given that even wild wolves take a whole lifetime to learn how to lead. One might just as well attend a weekend seminar to try to learn to be a good mother or a good CEO.

Learning leadership in a wolf enclosure is the worst possible approach. Anyone who wants to experience leadership qualities must observe wolves in the wild, in their natural environment. The family isn't led by the biggest, strongest or bravest wolf. Leadership is very individual. According to their abilities, other members of a wolf family can temporarily lead the group in certain situations. In the home territory, even young wolves do this. It doesn't make the alpha lose face.

Experience is important for the leadership of a wolf family. And if a wolf makes a decision in particular situations because of his experience and powers of persuasion, this is accepted by the whole group. So leadership is as individual as the personality that wields it. However, if a decision maker is needed, for example because a situation seems dangerous, it is the pack leaders who know, because of their experience, how to proceed.

Fundamentally, it is true that a leading personality should have mental strength and social intelligence, to be taken seriously by the members of the group. High-ranking animals always try to maintain a friendly underlying atmosphere and harmony within the family. This encourages solidarity and a feeling of community. Long-standing pack leaders don't need constantly to dominate anyone if they radiate natural authority.

For that reason an alpha position has nothing to do with aggression. Bosses who are forever boasting or being provocative are usually the ones who fear a loss of power, and for that reason are not leadership personalities. The wolf can set boundaries with its natural authority, for example with one single shot of direct eye contact or a growl or by blocking another wolf's path.

Incidentally, one study shows that the leaders in a group are the ones who suffer the most stress. In their scats (faeces) we find the hormone glucocorticoid, which is released during long-term stress. From an evolutionary perspective this means that a responsible position involves long-term, high social stress. This in turn can affect many areas of the body: weakening the immune system and reproductive system, and shortening life expectancy. So it is also in the interest of any good pack leader to maintain a harmonic and stress-free mood in the group. This is achieved by setting out clear tasks and boundaries and a precise framework for action, as well as practising rituals.

And as if we hadn't guessed this ages ago: leadership is female. A wolf family doesn't need a gender quota. The male and female pack leaders effectively make important decisions together, although in the event of doubt the wolf family, including the alpha male, takes its lead from the leading female. The males have no problem with that.

Some alpha females come from a long line of leading personalities. Very often the daughters of leading mothers also become leaders of the pack. They learn it from their mothers.

The parents of the pack usually stay together their whole lives. If one of them dies, their place will be taken by the next experienced wolf, which has already convinced the family of its social competence by making prudent decisions. Serious battles for a leading position within a family are extremely rare among wolves in the wild – unlike captive wolves. In more than twenty years of fieldwork I have experienced fatal conflicts for the position of leader on only two occasions. One was sensational, because an extremely dominant wolf was killed by her own family. A female pack leader of the Druids ruled her family with an iron fist. She chased her mother and one of her sisters out of the pack and behaved aggressively, particularly towards her other gentle sister, even killing her pups. After that I called the gentle sister Cinderella. The behaviour of the alpha female had a negative effect on the mood in the wolf family, which got worse and worse. The following year the dominant sister ran to Cinderella's den, presumably to kill her pups again. There she encountered bitter and violent resistance from the whole pack, which then killed her. Cinderella, whose six-week-old pups survived, assumed the role of leader. What happened next was amazing: the new alpha female adopted the seven puppies of her dead sister and the young of another Druid wolf. With twenty-one pups the pack had suddenly grown to twenty-nine wolves. All the family members showed an impressive empathy towards the young of their leader, who had made all their lives such hell. In principle it's hard for wolves to lose their leader, but here it had the opposite effect. The loss seemed to establish a sense of solidarity in the pack, which had previously been held together only by harshness.

Wolves have a strong need for harmony within their own family. The basic responsibility of a leader is to keep the family together and to unite them, not separate them – something I wish our own political leaders would bear in mind. Despots are extremely unpopular. Conditions under their tyrannical leader must have become intolerable for the Druids. So overnight the abused and oppressed Cinderella became a tolerant pack leader. The new couple lived peacefully together for many years until they died.

In the old days people used to talk about the 'alpha male' and 'alpha female' who led their pack and made all the decisions. These terms are long out of date and are no longer used in field-work. These days we talk about 'pack leaders' or simply 'parents'. The alpha concept comes from research into captive wolves. Alpha is the first letter in the Greek alphabet and represents the beginning, or number one. Beta is the second letter and omega the last.

For a long time it was impossible to observe the behaviour of wolves in the wild on the scale that we do today. In those days researchers believed that a wolf pack was a random collection of animals that came together in the winter to hunt large prey more efficiently. To gain a better understanding of wolves and to observe them more closely, they took them from various zoos and put them together in enclosures.

If you put social animals together as randomly and artifi-cially as that, they will inevitably compete with one another and in the end develop a kind of hierarchy of dominance, which is like the classic pecking order among chickens. Many scientists adopted the terminology and as a result went on spreading (false) information about alpha wolves. It took two decades before that was corrected and a new understanding of wolves was accepted.

The change in terminology reflects an important development in our thinking about the social behaviour of wolves. Today we know that captive wolves behave differently, and 'untypically'. They live like the inmates of a prison. In the worst case they have to get on with each other come what may, whether or not they can stand each other. Their social behaviour does not remotely correspond to that of a wolf family in the wild. They have no chance to migrate or mate with whoever they want; they're not allowed to hunt either. Anyone can imagine what that means for a group. What prevails is the traditional (prison) hierarchy of the alpha, who dominates and rides roughshod over the others, all the way down to the omega, the whipping boy, who in many cases suffers massive injuries.

I don't mean to condemn all wolf enclosures per se. There are some in which the social structure has been intelligently chosen, birth control is practised and the animals are hand-reared. I see it as quite natural that there should be enough room to hide and dig, as well as enough water for bathing. And yet in many zoos I see scarred and totally terrified omega wolves who have no possibility of escape and no possibility of being separated from the other animals. The answer of the director of an enclosure when I talked to him about an injured wolf, who said that it was like that in nature, reveals a frightening and culpable ignorance of the behaviour of the animals entrusted to him. In enclosures one can doubtless carry out brilliant studies into the body language of wolves, but not into their social behaviour.

A lot of myths have grown up about the position and tasks of pack leaders. Just to name a few: the alphas determine and control everything, they lead the hunt, they're allowed to eat first, and they're the only ones who mate. All of these myths can be contradicted by fieldwork studies.

Let's take the classic 'Only alpha wolves are allowed to mate'. About a quarter of all wolves in Yellowstone mate with different partners, with the consequence that several female wolves in a family have puppies – and sometimes bring them up together. If there is enough room and prey, nothing stands in the way of an increase in the numbers of the family. Evolution ensures that reproduction in a wolf family is assured even if something happens to its female leader.

On a single day during the mating season in February I once observed several female wolves in a pack mating with different males, even including one lucky fellow who had just dropped by in passing. The following spring four mothers had their pups in four different dens. Later, whenever the clan went hunting, they put all the pups in one den and appointed a babysitter. That represented a major saving in terms of 'staff', and more wolves who could be deployed for the hunt.

If there was ever a perfect pack leader in Yellowstone, it was the Druid alpha male number 21, whom you met in the last chapter. He defended his family completely fearlessly. I once saw him fight six attacking wolves and win. The biologist Rick McIntyre liked to compare him with Muhammad Ali or Michael Jordan: a unique talent with abilities beyond the norm. And for

Druid pack leader 21

a wolf a 'norm' isn't the average for a human being, because *every* wolf is a professional athlete.

Wolf 21 was a super-wolf. His parents came from Canada and had been reintroduced to Yellowstone in 1995. He was one of the first pups that came into the world after seventy years of absence in Yellowstone. At the same time, only a few kilometres away, his father was shot by a poacher. Biologists took the single mother and her young back to the special acclimatization enclosure where they had spent their first few weeks. When people entered the enclosure to feed the wolves, all the wolves fled to the furthest corner – except for our little super-wolf. He climbed on to a hill and placed himself between the bipeds and his family. Later, when he was released into the park with the other wolves, this pup was given a GPS collar with the number twenty-one. At the age of two and a half he joined the Druid wolf family, which had just lost its leader, and immediately became head of the pack. All the female animals were wild about him, and their pups loved the big fellow. He was always remarkably gentle with his fellow pack members. When he had made a kill, he immediately went away and lay down, leaving the others to eat their share.

Wolf 21 was a model leader with a lot of self-confidence. He knew what he wanted and what was best for his family. There was something calming for all the others about his aura.

The few moments when I saw him as dominant were during the mating season, when another wolf approached his partner. Then he would stand up and growl, or merely stare at his adversary. If he ran at his rival, the rival would usually throw himself submissively on his back.

A good leader is always a model for others. This pack leader had two outstanding characteristics: he never lost a fight and he never killed a rival. Once he had made his position clear, he demonstrated astonishing generosity and would let the defeated wolf live. Why did he do it?

In our human world, status is important for most of us. We want to be noticed and confirmed as a person. Social acceptance acts like a drug. It makes us so happy that we will do almost anything for it. Apart from the neurotransmitter dopamine, our brain also releases our own innate opiates and the hormone oxytocin – a hormone that ensures greater calm and trust. The more of these are released, the better we feel. In terms of evolutionary biology, high status is important for survival. Because if company or food are in short supply, the one with the highest rank has preferential access. So in the end it's all about reproduction. In evolution offspring that survive are the only currency that counts.

Sometimes we are forced by special circumstances into a position that we never wanted to find ourselves in. That can happen to wolves too.

You remember Casanova, who won the hearts of the female Druid wolves and was accepted into the pack as a result? Previously he'd been beaten up several times by the pack leader. The leader could easily have killed him, but he repeatedly let him go and finally accepted him into his family.

When the old Druid pack leader died at the age of nine, contrary to all expectations, Casanova let the post of boss pass to his younger brother. The handsome lady-killer was no use as boss. He was too easily distracted, and more interested in the girls than he was in the well-being of his family. He would rather be free.

Casanova didn't seem to care about his loss of power. He was much too busy with other things. Optimistic and in a good mood, he set off on his travels whenever the mating season approached, and generally distributed his genes among the neighbouring wolf families. After these amorous excursions he always returned to the bosom of the family. Essentially a lover, not a fighter, Casanova was still there when he was needed.

Regardless of whether it was a matter of driving strange wolves out of his territory when hunting or rearing the young, when things got tough, the family could depend on him. When things went bad, he turned up like the cavalry and helped wherever he could. But he never gave a hint of wanting to assume the role of leader.

But then, at the ripe old wolf's age of eight, Casanova had another surprise up his sleeve. Because all the bitches in his pack were related to him (wolves avoid incest), he returned to his former home territory. But this time he took five of his nephews with him and collected five females from a neighbouring wolf family. All of a sudden the wolf who never wanted to be a pack leader had a family of his own, eleven strong. Until his death in October 2009 he performed his task well – apart from the usual amorous excursions during the mating season. Casanova was the father of many wolves in Yellowstone. In the last year of his life he had pups in his own family for the first time. The little ones were the image of their father: black, big and very independent.

Casanova, the wolf who never wanted to assume responsibility, was now the head of a pack. Not everyone manages to undergo such a transformation, but many grow into the role. They learn, they become more experienced and – because they know the rocky way upwards – are in the end often the best leaders.

Are pack leaders always commanding and serene? Always cool, never making mistakes? No, of course not. Wolves sometimes end up in life-threatening situations. They are often surprised or overwhelmed by a situation and don't know what to do. Of course they can also react doubtfully. That doesn't affect their standing in the family. The Canadian biologist Paul C. Paquet sums it up when he stresses in his lectures that 'even pack leaders can be idiots'.

I've learned a lot about my own leadership behaviour by observing wolves. For example, I remember my first attempts at trying to be a 'leader'. To top up my earnings as an author, I spent several summers as a tour guide in the USA. Being addicted to harmony, of course I wanted everyone in my group to be happy. I decided to let the travellers have a democratic say in what we did. But at the question 'What would you like to do today?' or 'When shall we set off tomorrow?' they got into such fights with each other that I soon gave up my attempts and calmly got on with determining our daily schedule. And lo and behold – no more complaints, everyone was happy. Assuming responsibility for the trip and for my guests and confidently making decisions was hard for me at first. I learned how to do it from the wolves. As a 'pack leader' I made decisions on the basis of my authority and was accepted because my group knew I wanted the best for them.

The Strength of Women

What Connects Women and Wolves

One of my favourite questions, which I like to ask at every talk I give on wolves, is: 'If an important decision needs to be made for the pack, who do you think has the final say, the male or the female?'

I get the expected reaction; while the women grin and jab their elbows in their husbands' ribs, the men look wearily at the ceiling and groan, 'Yes, of course, just like at home.' I notice that times have changed in the younger generation when I give talks in schools, and in reply to my question the children shout in enthusiastic unison: 'Mamaaaa!'

And it's true. In a wolf family the parents decide together, but the really important decisions – such as how, when and where the pack goes hunting, or where the natal den is dug – are made, both by humans and wolves, by the highest-ranking female. In the end everything of any importance to the family is geared towards her. She is the one who binds one or several males to her with her sexuality, so that they will hunt for her and her offspring and protect them against enemies. She is the true centre of the family. Of course among wolves – as in every large family – conflicts arise between male and female animals. I have also known female wolves who have 'beaten up' the males, and vice versa. But in general conflicts are resolved regardless of sex or rank. For example, if a dispute between the young wolves has to be resolved, the wolf closest to the brawlers intervenes and tries to impose order. That could also be an older sibling.

Yellowstone has produced a lot of brilliant female wolves, but one of them was a legend even in her own lifetime – until her tragic death. Everyone who saw her was fascinated. For the biologist Rick McIntyre she was the 'Angelina Jolie of the wolf world'. We called her '06' (Oh-Six) because she was born in 2006. In a National Geographic film about her life she's called 'She-Wolf'. When she appeared in Lamar Valley at the age of two, we already noticed that she was something special. When a wolf leaves her home, her top priority is usually to find a partner and raise young. She-Wolf was in no hurry. Throughout the first winter she had up to five suitors during the mating season, which is very unusual among wild wolves. She rejected even the biggest and strongest contenders. Instead she took up with two young males, brothers, and founded a family with them.

Shortly after the birth of her first pups She-Wolf left her den and within ten minutes had killed two elk cows – all by herself. The males watched. In fact, it looked as if the female wolf was teaching the two inexperienced brothers how to hunt, exactly as she was to give all the other family members a kind of survival training over the next few years.

She-Wolf was one of the best hunters there had ever been in Yellowstone. Normally the whole pack takes part in a wolf hunt. Each one has their own task – driving, chasing, attacking – right up to the pack leaders who deal the final *coup de grâce*.

She-Wolf was different. She liked hunting alone, and also preferred fighting face to face. A bull elk can weigh between 300 and 400 kilos. When he is attacked he defends himself by trampling the marauder to death with his front hooves, or slinging them into the air with his antlers.

When hunting, She-Wolf always put herself in the most difficult position. Her hunting technique was masterful. She ran close beside her prey, jumped up, turning her head, and bit the elk's throat. She even managed to do that several times while swimming in a powerful stream.

Once I watched as she attacked an elk cow on the shore and fell down the embankment with her. The elk pressed the wolf's head under water, and She-Wolf let go of its throat and fought her way out from underneath it. Then, treading water, she pressed her victim's head under the water with all of her weight until the animal drowned within a few minutes. The problem she had then was that the dead elk, and thus the food for her family, lay in deep water. And again she surprised everyone who was watching: the wolf dragged her prey into even deeper water and let it drift to a sandbank before dragging the body on to it. She-Wolf knew exactly what she was doing, and planned strategically to feed her family.

Wolf '06' or She-Wolf, Yellowstone superstar

With her intelligence this wolf drove the most experienced biologists to despair. Doug Smith, the director of the Yellowstone Wolf Project and the biologist responsible for wolf tranquillizing and GPS collaring, said, fascinated: 'For three years I've been trying to tranquillize her from the helicopter, but she's always tricked her way out of it.' Normally the wolves run in all directions when they hear the helicopter. They can distinguish the noise of the single-propeller Cessna, with which the weekly inspection flights are made, from the sound of the helicopter in which the researcher sits with the tranquillizer gun.

She-Wolf usually didn't run away. She stopped and looked straight at the scientist with an expression of contempt: 'You're not going to get me!' Then the wolf fled among trees or behind rocks. It was only after three years that Smith managed to catch her.

In December 2012 She-Wolf made a fatal error when she left the protection of the national park for the first time and walked to Wyoming. It was the final day of the hunting season, and she was the last wolf to be shot that season.

When legends die, emotions run high. After the death of She-Wolf I received lots of emails and letters from people who had either seen the wolf with their own eyes in Yellowstone or had heard of her. Most of them were from women who had particularly identified with the charismatic wolf.

The world of wolves is a woman's world. I've established this in the many years that I've been working with wolves. Most of the fans and advocates of the big Canidae are women. Both at my readings and on my wolf tours men are in a distinct minority. Why might that be?

People react differently to wolves – just as wolves do to people. When I finished my ethology internship in Wolf Park in the early 1990s, one of the few men with permission to enter the wolf enclosure was the photographer Monty Sloan. He was a graceful man with a gentle, friendly air about him – by no means a macho guy. The wolves loved him. Whenever he went to see them they crowded around him to be stroked by him and to lick his face.

Every now and again, apart from us interns, wolf sponsors were allowed to join the animals in the enclosure to stroke 'their' wolf. One day a tall young man appeared, clearly someone who worked out daily in the gym. He had dragged a couple of friends along and boasted to them that he was going to show the wolves 'who the alpha is'. Only we could see the fine pearls of sweat on his forehead when he stepped with us through the doubly secured gate.

As always the wolves came charging enthusiastically towards us. We knew how to behave: feet placed firmly on the ground to keep our balance, enjoy the wolf kisses and scratch the animals on the belly. Then something unexpected happened. The wolves stopped abruptly in front of Mr Macho. Two of them froze and stared at him, the hairs on the back of their necks bristling and their ears pointing forward. They clearly found him weird. Wolves are excellent observers of body language. It's the only way they can correctly assess potential prey. This biped wasn't behaving the way they were used to. The animals were uncertain.

Mr Macho tried the cool approach. 'Hey, come here!' he barked at them abruptly.

The wolves jumped back and tucked their tails between their legs. Behind the fence his friends whooped with joy.

Meanwhile the pack leader had finished greeting Monty, and was suspiciously eyeing the new visitor. He approached him cautiously. In his typical wolfish way he 'tested' the young man by taking a corner of his jacket in his mouth and pulling on it. The guy made as if to tug the jacket away from the wolf, snapping, 'Stop that!' Anyone who has tried doing that with a 50-kilo wolf knows it's a waste of effort. The Wolf Park staff knew what was about to happen. The wolf would go on testing the guy, and eventually give him a good nip. They intervened and conducted him out of the enclosure. The wolves only calmed down again once he was out of sight. Why did they treat him differently?

Most women were fearless when they met the wolves. They were delighted. Did they recognize their own 'wolf soul' in the animal standing in front of them? Women have a different way of dealing with nature. They aren't afraid of looking vulnerable, and they don't want to 'conquer' as most men do. 'Wolf-conquerors' seem to believe that what other people think of them is more important, and in their opinion there's no need 'to humble yourself' or 'curry favour'. Except it doesn't get them very far; quite the contrary.

Mr Macho had approached the wolves threateningly, but also insecurely. He had bent over them from above and spoken to them in a deep voice. That doesn't just scare the wolves away; it wouldn't make such a great impression on most female bipeds either. Monty behaved quite differently. He spoke softly and gently to the wolves, knelt down and stroked them delicately. They loved him for that.

Time and again in my research in Yellowstone I see that it's the quiet, reticent ones who are lucky enough to see wolves at close quarters. And most of them are women or experienced wildlife photographers.

What fascinates women about wolves? Is it their wild, untamable aspect? Most women when dealing with animals have the gift of withdrawing, observing and waiting, while men tend to want to thrust themselves forward, to control and dominate. That's why there are so many more male bear fans than wolf fans.

The great German wolf researcher Erik Zimen once said to me, when we were talking about women and wolves: 'In history both wolf and woman have seemed to be the ones who were oppressed. But in reality they're the ones who are strong.'

★

Let's consider the role of women in the domestication of wolves, because in all likelihood without them there would be no dogs today. Many attempted explanations are male-oriented: wolves were tamed as hunting partners, for food in difficult times or to protect humans. During my work in the wolf enclosure I have brought up wolf pups. To socialize them, to imprint them in such a way that they trust human beings from the very beginning, a pup must be taken away from its mother at a very young age. We staff members were the human nannies for the little ones. We fed them from a bottle, cleaned them and slept tightly snuggled up with them at night. After a few weeks we took them back to their family. What we were doing was not domestication (that's a process that takes tens of thousands of years), but early imprinting. The little wolf pups, once they reached adulthood, weren't afraid of people, which made it considerably easier to feed them and keep them in the enclosure.

Would a man have been able to imprint a wolf pup to himself many years ago? Not at all. Because that meant feeding with milk, and at a time without livestock (sheep, cattle, goats and pigs were domesticated only after the wolf) that came only from women. So it must have been a woman who took a young wolf pup one day and gave it the breast. Perhaps because she had too much milk, or because she felt sorry for the abandoned, helpless wolf pup that she was holding in her arms. Without being aware of it, she sparked a revolution in the history of humanity. Because after the wolf came domesticated animals. The hunter became the herdsman. The course of history changed.

Perhaps in some sense even today we women remember our special role in evolution, which is why we have such a close relationship with wolves.

When I began working with wolves I often talked to Erik Zimen about the gender-specific difference in the assessment of wolves. At the time Zimen was researching a captive wolf pack in the Bavarian Forest National Park. When all nine of his wolves broke out of the enclosure, he experienced the reactions of the population at first hand. While the men (hunters, police, army) hunted down the wolves and killed them, the women appeared in the media begging for them to be allowed to live. 'The wolf isn't dangerous to humans; the human is to the wolf,' one of them wrote. Another got in touch claiming she had heard a wolf howling outside her bedroom window in Munich. In reply to Zimen's question of how she knew it was a wolf, she said, 'Because it sounded so beautifully eerie.'

If wolves show up in an area today, a lot of men respond with rejection. 'Away with them!' 'No room for them here!' In women, on the other hand, they often arouse protective instincts, pity and above all deep longing for the last remaining wild things in our time.

The ethnologist and psychoanalyst Clarissa Pinkola Estés is convinced that in every woman a wolf-woman slumbers, the guardian of the female primal instincts and intuitive knowledge of right and wrong. In her bestseller *Women Who Run with the Wolves* she writes that a woman can only be strong, healthy, creative, whole and happy when she gets back to the roots of her instinctive nature – the 'wolf-woman', the wild, untamed primal woman within her. To do that she must shake off the role of being sweet and nice and conformist, of obedience, compliance and submission.

Whether one agrees with this idea or not, the fact is that no species is socially so close to the human being as the wolf. Probably in awareness of this essential kinship, many indigenous peoples see the wolf as the ancestor and totem of their own origins. For several Native American tribes the wolf stands at the beginning of the world as the primal father or mother of their clan. By tradition the dynasty of Ghengis Khan, the great Mongolian ruler, goes back to a female wolf. And even the highly civilized Romans, according to legend, owe the foundation of their city to the selfless sacrifice of a female wolf. Obviously femininity as the origin of life and the wolf as the symbol of wildness are mythologically close.

In the end, in all myths and stories, the wolf always touches upon two related phenomena of human life: fear and domination. Man's fear of all that he cannot control and determine, of as yet untamed nature, of independent women and the wild wolf in the woods. And the woman's fear of the dark forest, the violent man and the big bad wolf. In former times this fear was not entirely without foundation, and it is easily fuelled.

This play with anxieties was expressed in narrative form in countless fairy tales and sagas. The Red Riding Hood story, for example, can be interpreted in this sense in many different ways, usually with more than a hint of sensuality.

Psychologically Red Riding Hood represents a young girl being seduced by an older man, who first devours the grandmother and later also the child. This may symbolically suggest a sexual assimilation. So the intention of such a fairy tale at the time was to teach girls not to talk to strange men. In the fairy tale, Red Riding Hood is seduced by the lustful wolf, but rescued by the hunter. Her fear, the fear of all women and girls, serves to justify the man's privileges. Anyone who is afraid of the wolf in the forest will not question the hunter and his work, the man and his masculinity. In this way competition is removed and dominance established.

What both the wolf and Red Riding Hood learn in the fairy tale stands symptomatically – at least archetypally – for the situation of women and wolves in the real world. Both experience man as hunter and ruler. Here, perhaps, lie the deeper reasons for the affinity between woman and wolf. Both of them seem at first sight to be the oppressed, the losers in history. In fact, however, they are the strong ones. Because they can overcome their fear, and then be truly free and independent.

The Wisdom of Old Age

Why We Can't Do Without the Elderly

Wolves in the wild don't usually live beyond the age of between nine and eleven, unlike captive wolves, which can live to be as old as domestic dogs, so to an average of about fifteen. Of course among wolves too, old age eventually takes its toll. As with us humans, there will be aches and pains. The eyes go, and one doesn't hear quite so well any more. And after a long expedition through the territory or an exhausting hunt, it takes older wolves longer to recover. They also have problems with the weather. Wolves like snow and the cold, and have difficulty in hot temperatures. For old wolves great heat is even more of a strain. In such conditions they spend all day lying in the shade.

There is also the fact that many wolves suffer increasing numbers of injuries during the course of their lives. Large hoofed animals like elk, moose or bison are good at fending off wolf attacks. The consequence for wolves is broken ribs and bones. Illnesses that the wolf has survived have a weakening effect and damage the teeth, so that, like an old human, a wolf hardly has any teeth left and is unable to grab and kill its prey.

This is where the 'family social system' comes in. Other

members of the group assume most of the animal's tasks, particularly when hunting. Wolves are extremely flexible, and adapt quickly to new conditions. But you can't demand too much flexibility from 'retired wolves', who were previously accustomed to grinding through their daily routine.

But unlike what happens so often in the world of humans, in the wolf world old wolves enjoy great respect, are lovingly supported and seen as highly prized members of the family. In territorial battles with rivals, the seniors are the trump card for a pack. Yes, you are reading that correctly. The wolf world is terrific, don't you think?

Even if they can't get very involved on the front line, old wolves are invaluable to wolf families, for example, when they are hunting. A pack with just one old wolf has a 150 per cent better chance of winning. But why? Old wolves are no longer physically fit, they take part in the hunt less often and have to rely on the young, strong pack members. Why are these packs so successful?

It is their experience that makes old wolves so valuable. They have often encountered rivals in their lives, they have seen their family members killed in fights, they have killed other wolves themselves. They will avoid a conflict that they don't think they'll be able to win, and thus increase their chances of survival. Having an experienced wolf in its midst means that the pack is able to take advantage of past knowledge. In that way, for example, a smaller pack can defeat even a larger one.

I had the chance to observe a remarkable example of this in Yellowstone. The leader of the Silver pack had grown old. A young wolf was trying to be accepted by the pack, but was repeatedly chased away by the boss. Then, one morning, the situation had changed. The young whippersnapper was suddenly the pack leader, and the deposed chief reacted entirely submissively. The young wolf allowed him to stay in the family, and treated him with great respect. He licked the older wolf's wounds when he was injured, and for the rest of his life the ex-boss remained a respected family member. It turned out that the entire pack profited from this. Because the old gentleman was a master in the difficult art of bison-killing.

A few days after the change at head office, the whole wolf family went hunting – apart from the young pack leader who, with all the excitement about the new responsibility, slept through the early departure. They happened upon a limping bison cow. Our senior wolf knew what to do. He ran off, grabbed her tail and allowed himself to be dragged along by her. That gave the other wolves an advantage, because the bison cow could no longer defend itself as it usually did. After it had freed itself, it ran into a cleft between two rocks, and only its horned head was free. That could have been the ideal defence position, had it not been for the old wolf. He took a very good look at everything, ran round the rocks and snapped at the animal's hindquarters. Every time the bison turned round in its hiding place to defend itself, the old wolf ran back round the rocks and everything started over from the beginning. He had leapt in automatically as pack leader. Under his leadership the pack killed the bison.

When the young pack leader had awoken at last, he howled for his family. They answered him, and he swam over the river to participate in the 500-kilo bison buffet. Having the old guy in the pack had paid off.

How do we deal with our old people in the human world? Do we value their significant quota of life? Do we take the time to look after them? The large family in which most people once lived until they died barely exists today. In our own times, our living situation often requires the elderly and those in need of care to be put in old people's homes and care homes.

Things are different among indigenous people. There the old are respected and asked to contribute to the decision-making process. Their advice is valued. I find it regrettable that in the present day old people often count for so little.

Luckily, however, in the world of work older colleagues are becoming increasingly important. The whole team benefits from having 'best agers' around. They have great knowledge and often decades of experience, which makes them a very precious piece of capital. They have mastered their craft, they know how things work, and they enrich projects with their experience. The ability to think strategically, argue logically and to share their knowledge rather than keeping it to themselves are further strengths. And to that we can add level-headedness and an overall understanding of work. These are all experiences and qualities that wolves value.

The Art of Communication

How a Shared Song Can Establish Trust

I have lived in wilderness areas for many years. I have often heard the song of the wolves, but it has never touched me as much as it did on that cold November day in 1991 when I first heard the chorus of wild wolves in the forests of Minnesota. I had just moved into a cabin in the middle of the territory of a wolf pack. Every now and again I saw one wolf or another darting across the frozen lake in the distance. I wanted to see how well I could speak 'Wolfish', and tried to make the Canidae answer by howling, so that I might be able to establish their numbers.

I stood on the shore of the lake and howled, then listened, shivered and waited expectantly. Sometimes the chattering of my teeth was the only sound in the gloom. Then at last came the sound I longed for. Out of the forest rang a single low tone that got slowly higher and higher. It crept through my innards and into my heart. The answer was coming from the other side of the forest. In the end wolf voices joined in from all directions. Dark and sonorous, or bright and hysterical, jubilant. And I was in the middle of it. It was as if I was in Verona, La Scala and the Met all at once. I focused all my senses and tried to absorb the song into myself so that I would never forget it. I was singing with the wild wolves in their territory. That was the greatest gift they had given me since the start of my 'wolfish' career.

The song of a wolf is one of the most beautiful sounds in nature, as far as I'm concerned. There are various reasons why wolves howl. They are telling competitors that this is their territory, calling to missing family members or a potential mating partner and strengthening their social relationship. Choral howling helps to reinforce family bonds.

I couldn't help thinking about this when I went to eat in a restaurant in Gardiner after a long day's observation in Yellowstone. As I waited for my burger, I studied the family sitting at the next table. They were parents with two children: a boy of about fourteen and a girl of maybe ten. They both had iPhones; the boy was holding two. They were all so busy tapping at their phones and reading messages or emails that they barely paid any attention to the food that was put in front of them. They stuffed it down without looking up for a second. After their meal they returned to work on their electronic devices with even more intensity. There was a ghostly silence at the table. Except when ordering, the family members hadn't once talked to each other. They were lost in their technology. There were no real conversations happening any more.

Wolves are masters of communication, even without electronics. They 'speak' with their bodies: with their eyes, their ears, their noses, the position of their tails, but also by marking and howling. Wolves' ability to communicate clearly and effectively is one of the reasons why they so seldom fight with one another. Communication is important to create mutual understanding and to establish trust.

In Minnesota I couldn't tell how many wolves answered me. When several wolves (or coyotes) howl, it sounds as if the forest is full of them. Each voice sounds different. In a scientific study from 2013, researchers were able to determine twenty-one different types of howling in wolves. Each species (timber wolf, red wolf, etc.) has its own dialect, and each individual animal has its own unmistakable tone. Thanks to this ability, human beings – and presumably also rivals – have the impression that a large number of wolves are replying. We bipeds are especially easily impressed and imagine the pack to be much bigger than it is – a clear advantage for the wolves.

The body language of wolves is comprehensive; threatening signals, such as growling, making a low humming noise, baring teeth, snapping, obstructing paths or nipping, are intended to prevent serious fights. Calming signals like averting the head, lowering the eyes, ignoring and prodding with the paws help to reduce social stress. Signals of reconciliation, such as touching, lying close together, running side by side, licking and nibbling at each other's fur help lead to better understanding and reconciliation.

One important means of communication in both wolf and human lies in the eyes. Like human beings the wolves see a direct stare as a threat. If a wolf looks down or away, it's a submissive or a friendly signal. A childlike open face is associated with playful intentions. In both species – man and wolf – changes in the pupils indicate emotions: joy, pain, fear, annoyance.

Wolves avoid direct eye contact because they are very cautious in their dealings with one another. When communicating they may constantly give each other brief looks, but they avoid staring directly for a longer period of time.

When lovers touch each other they often close their eyes as a sign of well-being. So do wolves when their partner nibbles them in social grooming. Touch is obviously a source of pleasure to them. They like touching one another at all ages. This applies particularly when the wolf mother or a babysitter is looking after pups, and during the mating season when couples are courting. Mutual grooming is an important part of the social life of wolves, an expression of care and affection towards one's partner. We see a similar reaction in our own pets. If we stroke our dog, our blood pressure drops and the bond between us is strengthened. The power and healing force of loving touch are also highly valued in medicine. Gentle stroking and massage have been demonstrated to lower a patient's heart rate, and in the brain the production of anti-depressant neurotransmitters, such as serotonin and dopamine, are stimulated and the oxytocin level rises. Touch conveys closeness and security.

Communication between loving lupine couples prompts a delighted sigh from most human observers. The courtship of wolves takes place all year. The pack leaders sniff at one another. Noses touch. The face, the ears, the neck and the shoulders are licked and nibbled. She places her paws on the back of his neck or his shoulders, which looks like a human embrace. When the mating season begins at the end of January, the male behaves as playfully as a puppy. He lowers the front part of his body, jumps at the female, wags his tail and tries to jump on top of her from the side or from behind. If she isn't yet ready, she may fight him off, 'play hard to get', or sit down. Only very few courtship attempts actually end in mating.

When I think about how many signals a wolf family uses to communicate among themselves – and also with others – I realize how pitiful we humans look in comparison. We communicate with language, gestures and mime, but why do we so often fail to understand one another? We rarely express ourselves clearly enough. Dog owners (and parents) know that the alpha and omega of a good upbringing are clear and unmistakable signals. Dogs pay less attention to what we are saying – they hear only blah blah blah – but *how* we say it. 'No' means 'no', not 'maybe', 'perhaps' or 'we'll see'. When we say 'no', we must mean it and express it.

If we often find it difficult to interpret the communication of other people correctly, it really isn't easy to understand that of wolves. Howling in particular causes difficulties for wolf researchers. In the 2013 howling study the various dialects of wolves may have been categorized, but the scientists had trouble discovering the meaning of the sounds, which doesn't surprise me at all. Tape recordings and a computer don't replace field studies. Researchers must go out into the natural world and look at the whole range of communication. Only then will they – perhaps – be able to understand howling. As the following example shows, it isn't enough to recognize which wolf is howling. We will only understand what they are saying to the others when we can see the whole picture.

I once observed a wolf family. Part of it was resting in the snow, the others were frolicking around. One big black wolf seemed to be uneasy. He stood up, lay down again and ran to his family members, who ignored him. Then he swiftly trotted up the mountain, disappeared into a bank of fog and reappeared. Again he ran down a little way, stopped, stretched his head high and howled. A short deep sound that slid up or down at the end of each howl. His family ignored him. The black wolf ran on and called again. This time a few wolves stood up and followed him. Soon the whole pack had vanished behind the mountain.

Why had the black wolf howled? What had he been communicating to his family? Was it a 'Now get your butts in gear and come with me!'? Was he hungry, or eager for adventure, or did he simply want company? Or did his howling contain specific information?

Today most scientists agree that emotions are the reason why wolves communicate by voice. They can distinguish the fine undertones in every howl and are able to tell them apart. In that way they not only recognize single individuals from a distance, they also know what mood the howler is in at that point in time. One thing all mammals (humans included) have in common is that excitement is expressed by a higher note. The black wolf was telling his family that he was excited. That was enough to make his fellow pack members curious enough to follow him.

There are all sorts of myths about the howling of wolves. Let's look at a few of them and see if there's anything in them. No, wolves don't howl at the moon, even though that image is often used over the credits of romantic films – or horror films. If they howl more than usual in the full-moon phase, it has to do only with the better lighting, which helps them go hunting, for example. Typically wolves agree to go hunting by engaging in a group howl.

And contrary to some claims, wolves can also bark if they're in a state of alarm and want to warn of danger. I've seen wolves going absolutely crazy when a bear came too close to the pups outside their den. The little ones were sent immediately into the den with a brief warning woof. And then off went the noisy attack against the interloper: hysterical screaming, screeching, barking, growling – the whole shebang.

They're barking not only in defence of their young, but also in defence of their territory. In that way, a few years ago, the Druid wolves had an almost one-hour long 'barking fight', which I watched with fascination from about 200 metres away. The Druids barked at some interlopers hugely, loudly and for a long time with brief intervals of howling, and the trespassers barked back.

Yes, wolves seem even to know the time: Wednesday, 3 p.m. is choir rehearsal. For a while there was a wolf family in Yellowstone that regularly started howling at that time of day. The explanation was simple. On Wednesday a UPS truck transported post and groceries to the remote towns of Silver Gate and Cooke City by the northerly park exit. As soon as the truck appeared in Lamar Valley, the concert kicked off. I never found out what actually made the wolves howl. Perhaps the engine had a particular sound that they liked and wanted to reply to.

At any rate I always knew when the post was on the way. Eventually another vehicle took over the deliveries and the howling stopped.

Whatever its meaning, humans are fascinated and enchanted by the song of wolves. The ecologist and author Aldo Leopold provided a fitting description: 'Only a mountain has lived long enough to listen objectively to the howling of a wolf.'

On my wolf tours in Yellowstone it was always a special moment when we heard the wolves howling. On the last day of one such tour we all climbed on to a hill from which we were able to look out over three wolf territories, some of which intersected: the territory of the Agate pack in the west, the Slough territory to the south and Lamar Valley with the Druids in the east. I had set up the spotting scope for the group. It was a perfect day with sun, a blue sky and crunchy snow. We looked in all directions, searching for the wolves. Then we heard howling behind us. About 500 metres away a grey wolf stood, howling his heart out. The reply came promptly from the other side of the valley. Then the third wolf group joined in. We were surrounded by a choir of wolf voices. We spun the scope around like a top to locate the sources of all the voices. The Agates were closest and furious about the strange wolves in their territory. Their howling turned into massive barking. The Druids were insulting the Agates, because after all they had been there first. And the lonely howler couldn't calm down. The wolves engaged in a singing competition for over an hour.

Everyone who first hears wolves howling in the wilderness is deeply moved. Many people cry. The sound seems to touch our soul, something deep within us. A mixture of awe, joy and fear. I'm grateful that I can share this sound with other people. I look into the eyes of those hearing a wild wolf for the first time and know that we are all still connected with nature, however dependent our lives are on technology.

The Longing for Home

Why We Need a Place Where We Belong

It was winter in the valley of the wolves. It had snowed in the night. I climbed on to a hill and looked for a spot that the sun was beginning to warm. I distributed my equipment around me and set up the tripod. I fixed the heavy scope to it. Then I put the binoculars round my neck and slipped the radio in one jacket pocket and my little digital voice recorder in the other. The work could begin.

And there they were already, the rulers of the valley; the Lamar wolves were patrolling the boundaries of their territory. They were deliberately following a trail. They stopped on a snow-covered boulder. The alpha pair stuck their noses deep in the snow and picked up a scent that seemed to be familiar.

Wolves can't only smell with their noses, they can also 'see' with them. Their skulls have millions of scent receptors, some of them in their mouths. The place they were sniffing at so intensely told them not only which wolf had walked along there, but also how long ago. The wolf's nose is omniscient.

Smelling the markings along the territorial boundaries gives the rivals information about how many wolves live here and

how big and strong they are. While within the wolves' core territory it doesn't matter who walks in front – after all, they know
their way around – when patrolling the boundaries the pack
leaders are at the head. All the others lag behind, as if to say:
'Mum or Dad will test the situation first'.

Wolves live in fixed territories, their home. Home means
protection, food and a safe place to raise offspring. To mark off
their territory from strange wolves, the pack leaders leave scent
markings at small intervals like the posts of a garden fence. They
do this with urine and scats, and by scraping. So that the scent is
scattered by the wind, the marking must where possible be
placed on an elevated spot, such as a rock or a tree stump. For
that reason they lift their back legs as high as they can. All
wolves in the pack are allowed to mark, but only pack leaders –
both male and female – are allowed to pee 'high'. The
lower-ranking animals urinate by crouching down, even the
males. The pack leaders mark alternately, which not only under-
lines their claim to the territory but also demonstrates a sense of
community. They are a unit.

To ration out their urine and mark out their territory at as many
points as possible, the pack leaders 'sprinkle' only a few drops at
strategically important positions, such as a crossing of forest paths,
and distribute them over the ground by powerful scraping.

The Lamar wolves moved on, noses to the ground. Then I
noticed a behaviour typical of cheeky young wolves. One of the
young males had stayed a little way behind. He was sniffing
intensely at a tree that his parents had marked several times before.
After a quick glance around to check that no one was looking, the
little fellow lifted his leg as high as he could. As he did so, he kept
a close eye on the pack leaders, who hadn't noticed the insult.
A quick scrape, and the little rascal ran on and joined the rest of
the group. I'm sure I saw his eyes flash . . .

★

In the wolf world it is all about finding your place in the ecosystem and surviving. A good wolf territory offers enough refuges and a reliable provision of food. The size of a territory depends on the available area, the number of wolves in the population as a whole, the number of prey animals and the stability of the pack. Wolves always choose a territory large enough to provide them with food over a long period of time. The more prey animals there are in an area, the smaller the territory. In central Europe, the average wolf territories cover between 150 and 350 square kilometres. In northern Siberia and northern Canada there are territories of over 1,000 square kilometres.

Every wolf territory consists of an 'inner territory', where the wolves spend up to two thirds of their time, something like their house and garden, and an 'outer territory' that corresponds to a walk or a trip to town. In normal circumstances wolf territories remain stable from year to year and from generation to generation, just as natal dens are often used for decades. Wolves bond so closely with their home territory that after occasional expeditions into unfamiliar terrain they prefer to come home as quickly as possible.

Younger wolves tend to migrate above all during puberty, when it is important to conquer new worlds – and ladies. However, some of them, who have travelled hundreds of kilometres in search of partners, end up finding their way back to their birthplaces.

They carry an image of their home inside them like a map. They know every tree, every crossing and every spring. They remember buried food stores, they deliberately take shortcuts and use familiar route networks, they know the best places to cross rivers, and have their special favourite areas. In winter those are often sunlit resting places on high slopes, and in the summer shady spots in a forest. Up until the age of about five months the pups experience an intense habitat imprinting by repeatedly following their parents and siblings through the territory. They get to know the boundaries, the scents and the form of the landscape. And of course the little wolves also learn early on that it is more energy-efficient to use man-made routes, such as roads cleared of snow, cross-country ski tracks or snowmobile paths. This knowledge is passed on culturally. The offspring 'inherits' the territory and thus also the hunting grounds of its prey animals. Wolves learn where food is easily to be had, sometimes in the form of unprotected sheep or calves, and which animals are best avoided because it can be painful to approach them if they are on the other side of an electric fence. They know where people dump their rubbish, and, for example, on the dumps around Rome they have discovered a love of pasta, leading Erik Zimen, who researched the Italian wolves for many years, to call them 'spaghetti wolves'.

What is home for us humans? For some it is the smell of freshly baked cakes, for others church bells on Sunday morning, for yet others it is people – friends and neighbours. All of this is familiar to us; it gives us identity and security. We all long for something consistent. Home gives us that stability. A Russian proverb says: 'Your home is not where you know the trees, but where the trees know you.'

Some indigenous peoples believe that it is important for our souls to be in harmony with our place of birth. In their view, as our bones and muscles form while we are still in our mothers' belly, they absorb an impression of the energy fields of the environment in which we are born. After that we are forever harmonically linked with our place of birth, regardless of where in the world we live. This connection helps us, they believe, to develop a personal identity, and makes us the people we are.

Wolves have taught me deep respect for my roots, my origins, and for the certainty of where I belong. For a long time I was a stranger at home; I travelled professionally throughout the world. Personally, too, my life was a constant search for the 'perfect place'. I lived for a long time in Santa Fe, New Mexico, and in Arizona, Alaska, Maine, Montana and Wyoming. Every time I thought I had found a home, after a few months I was seized by a longing that I couldn't explain and packed my bags again.

It was only as I grew older that the concept of home assumed importance for me, and I understood how valuable a social environment is. After I had seen everything and travelled everywhere, I realized that home is more than a place. It was where my family, my friends and my neighbours lived.

Today I don't really feel much like travelling any more. What's the point of a fleeting glance at Phoenix, New York or San Francisco, when I don't know the town I live in, or the mountains and trees outside my front door? I have grown roots. I feel deep familiarity with the buildings, the landscape, the plants and animals of my immediate environment. My desk stands in the room where I was born – almost in the same place. When I work here I have a warm feeling of safety, of having arrived. My great-grandparents and grandparents built the house I live in. My great-grandfather's initials are carved in the drystone wall that forms the foundation. Every time I look at it I'm thankful for the effort that my forefathers made to make a home, which is now also my home.

The place where I live is the suburb of a small town in the state of Hessen. Like everywhere in the world, in small towns you only belong to a place if you have lived there for several generations. I'm lucky that my great-grandparents lived here; I'm a native. In my town and the surrounding district there are castles and fortresses from the Middle Ages. When I sit in the garden in the summer, I look at the ruins of a castle from the fourteenth century. In Germany we have an ancient civilization; we take it all for granted and forget that this culture is etched in our genes. If we allow it to happen, we can feel a deep familiarity and connectedness with our home.

The Lamar wolves had moved on and disappeared behind the mountains. At marking spots the pack leaders had urinated and scraped. Possible interlopers can still perceive these traces for two to three weeks. Clear boundaries don't just offer security, they also save energy, because no one wants to be constantly arguing with the neighbours. Everyone loses in a fight to the bitter end.

The need to protect and defend home and family is extremely highly developed. Whether and to what extent they do that depends on many things, but most particularly whether there is enough room and food, and various wolf families can live peacefully side by side. Overlapping territories are used communally. A good hunting ground with an adequate density of prey animals and a safe area for natal dens is like a rising share portfolio that everyone wants to have. And if you've got something, you tend not to want to give it away. In this respect wolves are like human beings, and they become passionate defenders of their home if there is a danger that it might be taken from them. But border disputes with really deadly outcomes predominantly occur between wolf families that are unrelated. The inhibition against attacking relatives is naturally strong.

The most frequent cause of death among wolves (after humans) is territorial battles with rivals. Twenty per cent of all wolves in Yellowstone die in that way. Still, they fundamentally try to avoid confrontation, because all fighting represents a risk of injury and is a danger to one's own family.

If all warnings and markings fail to have their effect and the enemy attacks anyway, the clashes are almost always aggressive. In this case every pack tries to drive the competitors away and if possible to kill them. Incidentally, the dangerous-sounding growls and snarls that we hear in some film scenes of fighting wolves are edited in, an acoustic trick by the film industry to lend drama to a scene. In reality, deadly battles have a ghostly silence.

I once observed such a battle between two rival wolf packs, when a long-simmering feud broke out between the Druids and the Sloughs. Both wolf packs had always had their eye on a choice bit of territory: Lamar Valley. For many years it had been the home of the Druid family. They were born there, like their parents. In their glory days, when a pack of thirty-seven wolves moved through the valley, everybody held their breath at the sight of it. But then fate shuffled the cards. The Druids lost their pups to illness, and the Sloughs began to spread into Lamar Valley and drive out its previous owners. Two years later the time had come for a changeover of power.

I was standing at my observation spot precisely between the two packs. Eighteen Slough wolves were devouring an elk carcass and had no clue that sixteen Druids were on their way towards them. None of them had so far noticed the others. Then, all of a sudden, the Druids came flying over the hill, the alphas and a grey yearling in the lead, tails held high, hackles up. The Sloughs fled to the west. The Druid pack consisted of a few adult animals, though most of them were, however, very strong. Some of the young Slough wolves hadn't yet understood what was going on. They stood in confusion by the carcass. *Run!* I shouted to them in my mind. *Run for your life!*

The attackers fanned out in a line, swam through the river and dashed up the slopes. The choreography looked perfectly practised, except that they weren't following anyone's directions, just their instincts. They reached the first Slough yearling. I was surprised that they simply overtook it, and hoped that the others would also only be put to flight. But then the Druids grabbed the second yearling. They pounced in a circle on the unfortunate victim. It was soon over. They left the dead wolf and ran further west, still on the trail of the fleeing Sloughs. Luckily they didn't catch any of them.

The expelled wolves left the valley a few hours later. For a short time they had been the rulers of the best wolf territory in Yellowstone. Now they had lost their home and one of their pups. They withdrew into their old territory.

Hardly any other mammal defends its home as passionately as the wolf. But what makes one pack more successful in its aggressive encounters with its neighbours? Is it only the number of wolves? Does the larger pack always win?

There are different criteria that can decide victory or defeat in a battle, staying in the territory or being expelled, life or death. More wolves means victory seems to be the obvious theory. And, yes, it can be strategically important. If a pack has only one more wolf than the enemy, the chances of winning are distinctly higher. But another thing that is essential for the outcome of a battle is where it takes place: in the pack's own territory or in the territory of another pack. It's a version of the classic 'home advantage'.

But even more important is the sex of the wolves. More adult males are an advantage. That's why it's also easier for them to be accepted as 'immigrants' into an existing wolf family. The pack leaders know that a male can strengthen their family, even if he is a mating rival. And the most important criterion, as I have already mentioned, is age. Packs with experienced old animals have the best chances of defending their home.

In all clashes, however, there are often surprises, such as remarkably altruistic behaviour. I once observed a territorial struggle in which a wolf was attacked by the enemy pack. His little brother risked his life by running past the brawlers, attracting the attention of the wolves and interrupting the attack. They both escaped.

In another battle a wolf wasn't so lucky. He jumped into the middle of the fighting group and 'sacrificed' himself for his family. He was killed.

Why wolves do this is explained by the 'Hamilton' rule developed by the biologist William Donald Hamilton, according to which altruism among relatives benefits the one who does not behave in his own interest, even if he apparently gains nothing in return, or loses his life. In general, siblings have a genetic match of about fifty per cent. By saving his brother's life, the young wolf ensures the continued existence, and thus indirectly the transfer, of his own genetic inheritance. These examples show the strength of a wolf family: defending others without consideration for one's own life.

I'm Off Then

On Going Away and Arriving

Alan was a ten-month-old wolf from Saxony. He received his name on 13 March 2009. On that day he was out and about on his own. Presumably he picked up a few trails, dawdled around here and there, caught two or three mice, and wasn't expecting anything bad to happen when he suddenly stepped in a trap. He turned round and pulled, but there was no way of escaping. The thing clamped on his leg held him fast. A short time later the bipeds approached him. There was no time left for fear. A tranquillizing injection put him to sleep.

When the young wolf dazedly woke up, only a heavy collar reminded him of his meeting with the humans. He had slept through the scientific procedure in which his blood was taken, and he had been weighed and measured. Now he wanted to get back to the safety of his family as quickly as possible. He took an unusual souvenir home with him: a GPS-GSM collar made using the latest technology. The collar locates itself by satellite and transmits its position by radio to a receiver station in the Wolves in Saxony contact office in Lusatia in east Germany. The little wolf sent a text message to the biologists Gesa Kluth and Ilka Reinhardt.

But Alan had no idea about any of this. He was glad to be back at home. The young wolf stayed for a few weeks with his family, as the researchers were able to tell from his signals. Then he left home and set off wandering.

On his journey eastwards the young male first spent almost three weeks in north-east Poland, west of the Biebrza National Park, then ran through the Augustów Forest, where several wolf packs live, before crossing the border with Belarus. In June 2009 he was 670 kilometres north of his parents' territory.

Four months later the young male stopped in the border territory between Belarus and Lithuania. He had travelled over 1,500 kilometres between April and October, and was 800 kilometres away from home.

After that there were no more text messages from Alan. As there had been several error reports before the radio silence, the researchers assumed that the collar had stopped working. Alan had taken them along on his journey – from their home computer.

The pilot study into the outward migration and spread of wolves in Germany from 2009–2011 was sponsored by the Federal Agency for Nature Conservation with funds from the Ministry of the Environment, Nature Conservation, Building and Nuclear Safety. It was replaced by the current 'Wanderwolf' project. Its data provides information about the choice of migration routes, preferred stopping points, possible barriers and the causes of death for wolves leaving the Lusatian wolf territory. It is also intended to help us gain a better understanding of how wolves behave in a cultivated landscape, some of which is densely populated.

We know little about when and why wolves leave their families, where they go and why some of them are true pioneers while others prefer the security of the family. Some leave because there isn't enough food, others are forced out of the family by their parents, particularly in the mating season, when the atmosphere is tense and a younger wolf appears as a potential successor to the pack leader. Parents generally behave very tolerantly towards their offspring until the age of two. The family is a springboard for young wolves. They can decide whether and when they will leave them, and whether they later want to return to the bosom of the family.

Emigrating is always a risky strategy. You can easily lose your life. It tends to be young males and assertive personalities who are drawn abroad. Many young wolves instead stay at home and help their parents raise their younger siblings. From an evolutionary point of view it can be just as advantageous to look after one's siblings as to bring up one's own offspring. As we saw in the previous chapter, with the young wolf sacrificing himself for his family, selfless behaviour can be beneficial for reproduction (Hamilton's rule). This also applies to help in the upbringing of the animal's own siblings, because wolves are ensuring the transmission of their own genetic information, some of which is present in the genetic material of their siblings.

As in human families, among wolves there are adventurers who are drawn to travel and those who prefer the hotel of Mum and Dad. Some of them, like 'Casanova', move from one family to the next as ambitious suitors.

The rule of thumb is the less food there is and the bigger their own family, the more wolves move away. But then they have to find a territory that is suitable for them and not otherwise occupied. The usual arrangement is that a young wolf moves out at between two and three years old and meets a female with whom he settles down and establishes a family of his own. But until then life isn't made easy for the young wolf. There is strong social competition, and during the mating season in the spring aggression among wolves reaches its peak.

★

By the mid-nineteenth century wolves had disappeared from Germany. Since then individual newcomers have arrived from the east, but all of them have been killed. After the foundation of the GDR, wolves could be hunted there all year. Some individual animals still sometimes managed to cross the deadly border. It was only with the fall of the Berlin Wall and the reunification in 1990 that the wolf was able to freely enter the West, and they were placed under protection all over Germany. In 2000 the first German wolf pups were born. Since then there have officially been wolves in Germany again.

The German wolves emigrated from the east, newcomers arrived in France from the Apennines in Italy, and wolves from Spain, Switzerland and Austria settled in the rest of western Europe. The distances that wolves cover when migrating are as different as the animals themselves: some of them run into the neighbouring territory, some to the nearest wolf population and others travel several hundred kilometres. Some wolves become true pioneers, migrating far beyond the boundaries of their territory.

It was only with the invention of GPS collars that scientists were able to follow these great explorers. For the smallest distance that a wolf walks, a linear distance was calculated. But an animal seldom moves in a straight line, instead walking to and fro or sometimes staying in one place for a while. The distances that some long-distance travellers cover are enormous. In Minnesota a wolf with a GPS collar walked at least 4,251 kilometres, 498 of those almost non-stop.

In their wanderings, the predators also have to overcome difficult obstacles or take shortcuts. The Canidae are also capable of covering significant distances over frozen lakes or seas. For example, it is assumed that the wolves that moved from Finland to Sweden crossed the Baltic Sea in winter, a stretch of 150 kilometres.

Wolves that cover great distances are obviously walking in a goal-oriented way. We don't know why they do this. Are they looking for a particular environment or a new mating partner?

It is also possible that some individuals have a natural inclination to travel long distances. One of these I called Hinkebein, 'the limping one'. He was the son of the famous Druid pack leader 21, and was born in the spring of 2000 as one of twenty-one pups. I gave him the name because when hunting in his youth an elk had kicked him and broken his back leg, which never healed completely. And yet when he was two he embarked on his grand tour.

Hinkebein was a fearless wolf. Because every suitable wolf territory in Yellowstone was already occupied he kept on heading south to Utah, where he walked into a trap set by a hunter. By that time the limping wolf had covered 320 kilometres in only four weeks. He made the return journey to Yellowstone more comfortably, in a transport case belonging to the biologists. Would his pack take him in again? My worries were unfounded. His family welcomed their prodigal son, who now had a double limp because the trap had injured his front paw. That didn't stop him fending off rival wolves a few weeks after his return. Within a very short time Hinkebein was fully back in business. Because of his handicap, which he had for the rest of his life, and his black fur, he was easily recognizable in his family. His excursion made him even more famous. A lot of tourists from Utah wanted to see 'their' wolf. People were touched by his personality and his eagerness in supplying food for pups, hunting elk and defending the natal dens against bears. He did more for the pack than many healthy wolves.

A migrant wolf has several possible ways of founding a family of his own. He needs a partner, food and a territory that belongs to him alone. Things can get dangerous for him when a territory is already taken, because then he usually has to expel or kill a wolf that is already settled there – at the same time risking being killed or injured himself.

But he can also – like Casanova – seek a partner in a different wolf family, effectively making a place for himself in a ready-made nest. But he will only be accepted if he is not a mating rival for the male pack leader. Or he can settle on the edge of an existing territory and hope he will find someone there to share his life.

Ideally he seeks and finds a new territory where there are as yet no wolves. Presumably that was also the motivation of the first wolves who migrated from Poland to Germany. They came under their own steam, so to speak, and were not, as is often claimed, 'reintroduced'.

Where wolves are hunted, many territories come free. It is accordingly easier for immigrants to settle. That's why it isn't unusual for populations to recover completely within a few years once they have stopped being hunted.

If you observe wolves over a long period of time, you have to brace yourself for a few surprises, as we did in December 2002, when we 'lost' a whole pack of twenty animals.

Can a wolf pack even get lost? And if so, how often does it happen? The Nez-Perce pack had disappeared for the second time in two years. It hadn't been seen for a long time.

One might assume that a pack of twenty wolves doesn't just melt into air. The researchers spent hours looking for the bolters by plane and on the ground – in vain! This wolf family normally stayed in the inner part of Yellowstone. But here they had been neither seen nor located. They were clearly away from their normal territory.

Six of the wolves in the pack wore radio collars. On the ground they could have been located by radio if their approximate location had been known. Without a clue of that kind the collars were no use. We just had to hope that someone would see the wolves and inform the biologists.

The Nez-Perce wolves had always been adventurers. In autumn 2001 they disappeared from Yellowstone and reappeared again in Idaho, about 200 kilometres to the east. The wolves had killed a dog and caused a great deal of excitement for several days. Then they ran back to Yellowstone and settled in the northern part of the park. Now, over a year later, they had disappeared again. The scientists looked for reasons.

The last location of the wolf pack was also the territory of three other wolf packs. The elk and bison population had decreased there. So not only were they short of space, their food had run out. That might have prompted them to migrate again. But where to?

In Yellowstone National Park, with its area of 9,000 square kilometres, almost every usable territory with enough room and food was occupied by wolves. The scientists hoped that when they found the Nez-Perce pack they would discover other so-far-unknown wolf territories.

After three weeks of waiting and searching there was still no trace of the animals. The biologists had to endure a lot of mockery, because who in God's name loses twenty wolves? Then at last, on 28 January 2003, the report came in: the wolves had been found in the National Elk Refuge in Jackson, Wyoming, adjacent to the Grand Teton National Park, very near Yellowstone National Park.

The biologists should have thought of that straight away. Every winter several thousand elk migrate to this reservation because – following an old tradition and as a tourist attraction – they are fed. Wolves had first discovered this land of milk and honey in 1999. Somehow the Nez-Perce must have got wind of this and set off in that direction, because they were discovered by plane right in the middle of this refuge. Because of the mild winter the rangers still hadn't started feeding the elk, so the wolves were living in the territory of an elk herd. Can anyone blame them for running away?

Two months later, at the end of the winter, they were back in their original home hunting ground in Yellowstone as if nothing had happened.

There are many scientific studies into the migration habits of wolves. One mystery seems to remain unsolved – *why* wolves undertake such long journeys when it is not about mating or food. Researchers try to answer this question by fitting GPS collars to the animals. I'm ambivalent on the matter. On the one hand, I can see how useful it is. For example, if you want to show whether a particular wolf is repeatedly and deliberately approaching humans or livestock, then you can identify the miscreant. Apart from that, I use the radio frequencies of the collars in Yellowstone myself to find the wolves more quickly. And yet I think that the cumbersome devices with the heavy batteries bother the animals and also inhibit their behaviour. Some wolves rebel against them. I know of at least three wolf packs that have chewed off the annoying appendages again and again. As a response to this clear act of rejection, the scientists developed radio collars with steel fittings. When these were bitten by the wolves they were stabbed by spikes. How far do we want to go? How much respect and dignity do we want to grant wolves and all other animals that are being scientifically researched? Is the information we receive worth the impairment of the life of a wild animal? If so, we need to go on asking ourselves how many animals we should track, what information we need and whether it is in the end useful to the animals.

Back to the long-distance travelling wolves and the question of *why*. On the basis of what I know about wolves so far, I don't doubt that there are adventurers among them who – for no bio-logical or scientific reason – just set off on their travels as if to say: 'Let's just see what's beyond the horizon.'

Do we always have to explain everything, or isn't it enough simply to keep our eyes open and listen to our emotions? Perhaps I think that way because I myself am an adventurer at heart, and can therefore put myself inside the heads of the wolves who go travelling.

Our German wolf Alan remained missing. After the last signals from Russia he could no longer be located. So in the end we were left with the hope that he had found a suitable companion in his new home and established a family of his own with her – and that maybe he will come back with his offspring one day.

Almost Best Friends

*How in Spite of All Your Differences You
Can be a Perfect Team*

Like many people who love wolves, I got into them through
dogs. I grew up with a German shepherd who at least looked
outwardly like a wolf. Axel was a trained guard dog and kept an
eye on me. Above all he was my playmate, friend and confidant.
I often crept into his kennel and slept cuddled up with him.
Even as I was growing up I couldn't imagine a life without dogs.

Humans and dogs as best friends. That social and emotional
proximity between two very different species is something
special. But it's not unique.

The longer I have spent observing wolves, the more they
have startled me, particularly where their relationships with
other species are concerned, such as the millennia-old friendship
between wolf and raven. They are completely different species
of animal, highly intelligent, family-oriented and social, and
share not only work but also a miserable reputation.

It was formerly believed that wolves socialized only with their
own species. Far from it. Vast as the difference between wolves
and ravens might be, they still have a very close connection.

When I organize wolf tours in Yellowstone and we are looking for wolves, I give my group tips on what to look out for. 'Watch very closely how the elk behave. If they lie in the grass, perfectly relaxed, there are no wolves nearby. But if they stand closely pressed together, all looking in one direction, you can assume that a wolf or some other large predator is heading towards them.' We don't look directly for wolves, and instead study the whole environment and most of all the behaviour of the prey animals.

One piece of advice always causes confusion: 'If you are looking for wolves, you must look into the sky.' I point to a spot in Lamar Valley, from which large numbers of ravens are flying up and landing again. There is a dead elk cow lying in the grass.

'Wait to see what happens,' I say.

The carcass is still untouched. The ravens have no way of opening it with their beaks, because the animal's fur and skin are too thick. They need help. But the cheeky birds also suffer from neophobia, which means that they are afraid of anything new, and therefore move only very carefully towards the dead elk. They hop nervously closer along the ground, they leap up and beat their wings, peck quickly, hop away again and strut busily around in their black suits. They do that until the carcass of the animal is proved to be harmless and an old raven settles on it. Once the animal has been 'declared dead', one of the birds starts calling. The whole troop flies over in response to his call.

Usually we don't have to wait for long. The alarm calls have done the trick, and within a very short time a few wolves come running out of the forest and open up the body of the elk, to the delight of the feathered flock.

Experiments with the carcasses of elk killed by human beings show that ravens won't touch them. But when they see wolves taking down a prey animal, they eat immediately. Wolves are also cautious with prey that they themselves haven't caught, and prefer to leave it alone. So ravens and wolves trust one another. Perhaps somewhere in the genes of both species there is still a memory of poisoned meat with which human beings in former times eliminated undesirable hunting competitors. The key to this relationship is familiarity. Raven biologists explain this with a possible 'genetic fixation'. Wolf and raven have evolved together over millions of years. The feeding cries of ravens may originally have been cries of frustration, because they weren't able to open up a dead animal without help. A wolf who happened to be passing learned this cry means that ravens have discovered a carcass. In turn, the raven understood that if it went on screeching, a wolf would come and help it.

If you observe ravens and wolves together, you establish that the birds behave differently towards the big Canidae to the way they do with foxes or coyotes, for example. There seems to be a degree of knowledge and tolerance between the two species from which each one profits. In eighty per cent of cases, a successful hunt by wolves will be accompanied by ravens, that is, they fly over the predators or wait nearby until the hunt is over and they are able to join in and eat. On a hunt by coyotes they only do this three per cent of the time. From this we may conclude that ravens distinguish deliberately between coyotes and wolves. Because they know they need wolves to turn an elk into a satisfactory meal, they remain constantly in the vicinity of the big predators. Whether they are setting off on a hunt, sleeping or playing with one another, the black Corvidae are always close by.

If the wolves summon one another to the hunt by howling, their winged companions react just as excitedly as my Labrador bitch when she hears the rattle of the food bowl. From the point of view of ravens, the howling of the wolves means that the table is about to be laid.

When the wolves have taken down an animal, the big feast begins. The ravens aren't afraid of diving in among the quadrupeds and stealing their food. The wolves are so busy stuffing themselves that while they may snap briefly at the tiresome thieves, they won't be kept from their meal.

If the wolves didn't quickly bolt down as much meat as possible, presumably there would be nothing left the next day. A single raven can devour up to two pounds of meat, or put it aside for a rainy day. With an average of twenty-nine ravens per kill, that makes for a lot of meat.

That's also one of the reasons why wolves hunt in packs. Not, as is often assumed, because that is how they can kill larger prey animals, but so that competitors for the food don't have a chance. Only then is there enough meat left for the young.

When the wolves are lying down to digest, the coast is clear for all the other scavengers, particularly coyotes, magpies and eagles. In this way a large carcass can be completely stripped within a few hours. So it is a mistake to claim that wolves need five kilos of meat per day. This figure ignores the fact that up to fifteen different species feed on a single carcass. We may assume a realistic amount of between one and a half and two kilos of meat per wolf per day.

Now the big game of hide-and-seek begins around the dead elk cow in Lamar Valley. The ravens keep a close eye on what the wolves are doing. When one of them buries meat, they sit directly beside the wolf and watch. Once the wolf has gone away, they dig up the meat in a flash. By depositing their stolen food high in the trees, the birds clearly have an advantage over the wolves.

Then the competition appears on the scene. The first grizzly heads straight to the feeding place. Now the wolves bolt down the meat even more quickly, before withdrawing and lying in the grass a few metres away from the bears. In Yellowstone in the summer, almost all prey animals killed by wolves are appropriated by bears within a very short time. The Canidae haven't a chance, and all they can do is wait and hope that their competitor will sooner or later have had his fill.

The grizzly makes himself comfortable on the carcass for the next few hours, all four paws stretched out. Meanwhile, about twenty ravens try to steal scraps. While the wolves remain at a respectful distance, the bear does his very best to drive away the irritating birds. With great swipes of his claws, he tries to bat them away as if they were horseflies.

Watch, learn and draw conclusions! Human, wolf and raven might have got to know each other like this in prehistoric times. In search of food, primitive man kept a lookout for wolves, since they provided enough meat for everyone. And the ravens helped him to find the wolves.

According to an ancient saga, Odin, the Nordic god of war, was guided by his ravens Huginn (thought) and Muninn (memory), as well as the wolves Geri (the greedy one) and Freki (the hungry one), on to the battlefields to devour the bodies of the fallen, whose souls were carried by the valkyries to Valhalla. All together they were a human-wolf-raven pack. The famous raven researcher Bernd Heinrich wonders whether the Odin myth describes a powerful hunting culture that we once possessed before giving it up in favour of agriculture and animal husbandry.

Many of the indigenous inhabitants of Canada and Alaska traditionally live in clans named after animals with which they feel connected. Humans who feel kinship with a clan of wolves or ravens see the black birds or the wolves as fundamental components of human culture. Even today, ravens are described as the 'eyes of wolves'. Sitting high in the trees, the birds can quickly spot dangers. Using special cawing sounds, they communicate both with each other and with the wolves.

Ravens produce a total of 250 different sounds, some of which wolves seem to understand; they almost seem to have a kind of common 'language'. With an I've-discovered-food cry, ravens draw wolves' attention to undiscovered carcasses or injured prey animals. A special there's-danger-on-the-way cry warns about bears or cougars approaching a wolf's den. That way wolves have more time to take their pups to safety.

In Banff National Park in Canada, the German wolf researcher Günther Bloch observed the collaboration between wolves and ravens when they discovered a carcass. Some time before they reach the body of a dead elk, the wolves wait for the ravens to spy out and properly check the carcass and the territory. As this happens, they observe precisely how the ravens are behaving. Both species always factor in potential disturbances and possibilities for escape. Everyone knows how much time they have before an undesirable competitor becomes a threat.

If there is a risk of danger – if, for example, a human or a bear approaches – both wolf and raven make use of several different possible escape routes. They usually flee the first few metres hectically and quickly. Then they tend to run into an area of forest or some other familiar terrain where they find shelter.

Sometimes ravens fly only to the nearest treetops. They wait there as the wolves observe the uninvited guests suspiciously from the edge of the forest. Sitting out potential dangers can sometimes be an effective strategy. At any rate, it's energy efficient.

The intelligence of ravens can be compared with that of chimpanzees. Every winter in Yellowstone I see how intelligent the black Corvidae are when the ravens loot the saddlebags of snowmobile drivers by opening the Velcro fastening with their beaks. These days the park service warns tourists against leaving their snowmobiles unattended.

Peace has returned to the scene around the carcass in the valley. The tubby grizzly has moved out of sight. The wolves lie sated in the grass, gnawing on little scraps of meat. The ravens have become bored. They start playing their favourite game: annoying wolves. A team of two ravens is getting on the nerves of a wolf that is lying apart from the rest with a little piece of meat and wants to be left alone. The birds keep hopping closer and trying to pick at the meat, which leaves the wolf far from impressed. Then one of the ravens runs at him from behind and pulls his tail. The wolf turns round to look at the bird, and its pal collects the coveted scraps of meat and flies off.

I saw the best show once. Several ravens, a coyote and a bald eagle were feeding from a carcass. The coyote was trying in vain to chase away the ravens. In the end it took a piece of meat to eat in peace some way away. A raven followed the coyote, repeatedly pulling its tail, until the coyote turned round to the troublemaker and dropped its food. At that moment the eagle plunged from the sky, grabbed the meat and carried it off. I will never forget the expression on the face of the coyote, which watched the bird with a mixture of rage and bafflement.

The tactic with which ravens torment their four-legged mates is finely calculated. They know the predators' body language and react differently to each of them. Wolves that exhibit dominant behaviour are irritated less often by the ravens, while they will attack wolves that approach a carcass in a submissive position by dive-bombing and pecking at them. The ravens clearly know which wolves will let them get away with bad behaviour.

The trust between ravens and wolves begins in their youth. Bernd Heinrich describes ravens as 'a kind of pet for wolves, which go hunting with them, interact with them and test what they can afford to do'. Often ravens build their family nests right beside wolf dens, moving back in every year, or rebuilding them year after year – if possible with a direct view of the dens. There all raven and wolf young engage in a unique process of imprinting and socialization that leads to lasting relationships.

Even when the pups are still in their natal den, adult ravens will approach the entrance and look curiously inside. Other members of the raven family are constantly busy picking up wolf scats or bone remains and carrying them to the nest.

At the age of about three to four weeks the first wolf pups come tumbling out of their dens, carefully observed by the ravens. First the puppies get to know all the members of their respective wolf clans: parents, aunts, uncles and siblings. Soon after that they meet their very personal 'in-house' raven faction. From that point on the wolf pups are constantly with the birds. They don't just see the ravens, they also store the smell of their feathers in their brains.

After the pups and ravens have met one another several times a day, they are soon romping around together. They play with each other, steal food from each other or practise feigned attacks. The ravens are at first superior to the pups. The fact that they like to tease the pups by nipping their fur, pulling their tail or briefly shooing them away is part of their daily entertainment schedule. The ravens could injure the wolf pups with their powerful beaks, but they mostly behave very gently. They seem to be testing how close they can get to the little wolves, and how quickly they move.

Later the roles are switched and the pups move from being the hunted to the hunter. When ravens approach, the little wolves stalk them and try to jump on them. In that way birds and wolves become familiar with one another.

For wolves ravens are not just alarm systems, annoying dining companions or playmates for the kids, they are also, by eating the wolves' scats, the 'clean-up team' for the den area. The scats of adult wolves often contain bones and hair, which are excreted undigested. Ravens peck at this waste matter and fish out the edible parts for themselves. They eat the pups' faeces whole.

When the adult wolves return to the den from hunting, they regurgitate predigested food for their pups. The ravens use that moment to steal the meat from the inexperienced little ones. Some birds even follow the wolves from a carcass to the den in expectation of a warm and ready-chewed meal.

Even when the predators are grown, the impertinence of their feathered companions does not abate. I often see ravens tormenting resting wolves. They peck at their tails or paws. Normally the irritated wolf stands up and goes and lies somewhere else. This irritation also shows the ravens how individual wolves behave and where their tolerance boundaries are.

Once I observed a touching scene. After the Lamar wolves had eaten from a carcass, they lay down in the snow for a siesta. Suddenly I noticed a dead raven between the paws of a wolf. Who had killed the bird and how it ended up there I don't know. When the pack set off, the female wolf with the bird ran to the river and laid it on a piece of ice. When the raven slowly slipped into the water, she watched it, tilted her head to one side and then to my surprise dived head first into the water. She came back up with the bird in her mouth. What now? Clearly she was looking for a hiding place for it. She found a little cavity in the snow. Carefully, almost tenderly, she laid the raven inside and pushed snow over the entrance with her nose. Only then did she follow her family. To me it looked as if she had been burying a 'friend'.

If it's possible in nature for different species to live together for their own advantage and be friends, why is it so hard for us humans to come to terms even with representatives of our own species with different origins or skin colour? Ravens are the perfect example of successful inclusion.

Planning for Success – the Wolf Method

Why It's Important to Have a Plan

Junior had big intentions. For the first time in his life he wanted to go hunting on his own. His parents had been preparing for it for months, showing him when it was important to be quiet, how to creep up and test a herd for weak animals, when to pounce and how to kill. At the same time he had observed the adults very closely and even killed the occasional hare on joint hunting expeditions with them. The one-year-old wolf seemed to be full of enthusiasm.

What he hadn't taken into account was that the prey he was creeping up on with slow, stiff movements wasn't an elk, but a peacefully grazing 700-kilo bull bison. Junior very cautiously approached the bison until he stopped only half a metre from its hindquarters. The bison was looking in the other direction and, apparently, hadn't yet noticed his stalker.

The young upstart paused. He had crept up on his prey, and now clearly didn't know what to do next. He briefly glanced back to the den area, but no one from the family was there to help him. So he just stood there.

Perhaps the young fellow moved or the bison smelled him,

because it slowly turned its massive head round and looked at the yearling. Then, unimpressed, it turned its head back to the front and went on eating. A short time later the bison was bothered by a fly, and it flicked its tail right in front of the little wolf's nose. Startled, the wolf spun on his axis, wedged his tail between his legs and fled for dear life.

He hadn't yet learned how to approach a hairy bison monster. It was only with a lot of practice, play and above all constant observation of the experienced older wolves that he would be able to perfect his hunting techniques over the months that followed. At first the odd experiment would backfire, but a few years later Junior became the leader of his own pack and an excellent hunter.

Lamar Valley in Yellowstone is a paradise for observing interactions between wolves and their prey. In the winter, deep snow drives the prey animals into the valley, where the grey hunters are waiting for them.

I've witnessed many hunts, from the attack of a lone female wolf on a wapiti – the American version of the European red deer – in a raging torrent, to the attempt of a pack to catch quick-running pronghorns and an elk hunt by thirty-seven (!) wolves, which left all observers breathless. The survival capability, persistence and strength of the wolves are far greater than those of human beings. Again and again the predators have to adapt to prevailing circumstances and the species in the area, because they're not the only ones who are familiar with their territory – their prey animals are as well. Like the wolves, they too have their own special places; when wolves go hunting, that's where they head for. Their hunting strategies differ according to habitat and parental family culture. They learn hunting from their parents and also pass on these techniques to their offspring. The weather conditions and the defence strategies of their prey are crucial to the success of a hunt.

They organize their attacks like a military unit, because they know that it isn't just a waste of energy – it's also dangerous to run off without a plan. That's why risk assessment is an important element. In the end it's about killing without being killed yourself.

Wolves must also observe their prey very closely. They perceive the smallest changes in an animal, even when it is only one of many in a herd. They see things that we wouldn't notice: a limp; heavy panting.

I got a hint of this when I was doing my internship in the research facility of Wolf Park. Several wolf packs lived there, and a small herd of bison. Every Sunday when visitors were allowed in, several wolves were led to the bison. As a rule these encounters were unspectacular, because of course only healthy bison were brought along to this presentation. The wolves circled the bison once or twice and searched in vain for a point of attack. The herbivores were strong and in good physical condition. The wolves hadn't a chance. They dawdled away.

This hunting behaviour is an innate instinct that the wolves don't lose even after several generations in captivity. Only once did it look as if they were going to be successful. For almost half an hour they circled a bison, and tried repeatedly to attack it. It was only when the animal developed pneumonia a week later that we knew that the wolves had noticed its weakness a lot earlier than we had.

Through constant surveillance wolves don't just test physical defects, but also the psychological state of their potential victim. Some prey animals don't seem to be able to survive the concentrated gaze of a wolf for very long. They break away from their group and run off, which can be fatal for them.

In Yellowstone the preferred prey animals of wolves are wapiti*, also called elk. They provide enough food for a complete

---

* In Germany the preferred prey of wolves are red deer, roe deer and wild boar.

wolf family for several days, and yet they are not as dangerous as a bison. A timber wolf weighs between 50 and 70 kilos. A bull elk weighs about 350 kilos, an elk cow 240, a calf just 100 kilos – and a bison almost a tonne.

Would you fight someone six times as big as you? That's exactly what a wolf is doing when it attacks a wapiti bull. Without a clever hunting strategy nothing is going to work. The strategy consists in observing the chosen prey, creeping up, testing and attacking. I have seen wolves standing on their back legs like rabbits to peer over a hill. Or they will hide in the bushes or behind a rock and wait for their victim. In the summer they creep on their bellies through the tall prairie grass to get closer to the prey. Like a cat, they can freeze their movements with every step. When the elk look over to them, they become perfectly still until they look away again. The tactic is to get as close as possible to the prey without being noticed before the hunt begins.

In the event of an attack, the normal reaction of elk is flight. If they stay close together, the wolves lose interest within twenty to thirty seconds. But if the herd separates, the predators will almost always pursue the smaller group. If the wolf pack is a large one, it usually splits up and chases the different groups of elk independently. A wolf hunt may appear disorganized to outsiders, but it isn't. The wolves don't just look for signs of weakness in their prey, but constantly observe one another. By doing so, they can rapidly and efficiently check out any number of potential prey animals. Success is close when only one or two animals from a group of elk are left at the end.

When wolves attack elk calves that are only a few days or weeks old, there is rarely a chase; instead, they dart forward, grab the calf and pull it away from its mother. The wolf must 'work' round the cow to get to their prey, and of course the mother will do everything she can to defend her calf.

With a fleeing elk, the most dangerous place is right behind or in front of it. A kick from a sharp-edged hoof can seriously injure an attacker. That is also why most attacks are carried out by at least two wolves, which run by the side of the elk and snap at their hindquarters. The idea is to injure the prey and weaken it through loss of blood. A direct bite to the throat is too dangerous. Calves and other prey animals, on the other hand, can be killed by a throat clamp, which suffocates the victim.

One popular hunting method among wolves is ambush. One wolf runs ahead and hides, while the others drive a group of elk towards it. At the last moment the wolf jumps out of hiding and attacks.

But prey animals are capable of defending themselves as well. Towards the end of the winter, when the bulls have lost strength as a result of the cold and the rutting season that preceded it, they don't flee, but stand up to their attackers. For the wolves, that means avoiding antlers and hooves.

Elk cows like to flee into water. Here, with their long legs, they have a better footing, which doesn't prevent some wolves from killing their prey while swimming, which was the speciality of She-Wolf, as I described in the 'Strength of Women' chapter.

I once watched, fascinated, five wolves hunting an elk cow. She was grazing on the valley floor, and I only noticed them when she looked up and stared with great concentration at something that was moving towards her through the mountain sagebrush. Wolves! In front of my eyes, the 'dance of death', millions of years old, developed between wolf and elk. A carefully choreographed ritual between attackers and prey. A series of predictable actions: seek, approach, observe, attack, kill. Even the steps of the cow were predictable and showed me what would happen next.

There are various 'dances' by an elk which show the wolf and the experienced observer what condition the animal is in. A healthy, strong elk keeps its head held high and thrown slightly back. That gives it a better all-round view. With a light, slightly exaggerated-looking trot, they look like Fred Astaire dancing through the rain. Others demonstrate their strength by leaping stiffly with all four legs, rather like cheerleaders do. This is an almost provocative way of saying 'You're not going to get me'.

By watching the 'dance' of their prey, wolves can see how good their chances are of taking it down. Often, after the little demonstration of their capacity for action, the elk stop and stand up to their attacker, who usually flee the sharp hooves and retreat.

The cow I was now watching went into a full gallop, her head stretched forward. All the wolves set off after her. Normally a fit elk can escape a wolf thanks to its long stride length. But this was not a healthy animal. The wolves quickly reached their prey. The cow shook them off, kicked out with its front hooves and struck one of the attackers. He rolled through the snow, struggled to his feet and continued with the hunt. The wolves clung to their prey and wouldn't let go. Their victim stumbled and fell, two wolves at its throat, one at its belly and two on its back legs. Once again it tried to stand up. Then it collapsed once and for all.

Seeing wolves tear a big prey animal apart isn't a pretty sight, and not for those of a sensitive disposition. Watching some scenes I have to remind myself that wolf pups are waiting for their food.

One wildlife cameraman once told me that in many nature documentaries the act of killing is cut out of consideration for the audience. This means that viewers have a prettified and unreal image of the hunt. The shock is all the greater when they experience it live. I've seen tourists throwing stones at a grizzly bear because it had killed 'poor Bambi'.

For that reason, before my wolf tours I always organize a

meeting to prepare those interested for what they are going to see. I show them scenes from films, including shots of a hunt. One participant furiously complained to me afterwards. No, she didn't want to see that – wolves tearing animals apart! She cancelled her booking.

Nature isn't a Disney film, even if that's how we'd like to think of it. Death can sometimes be bloody and horrific. Much crueller, in my view, are factory farming and animal transports. Wolf hunts are a part of nature, and neither wicked nor brutal. When I see the wolves' faces appearing out of a carcass after a successful hunt, exhausted but happy, and with blood-drenched jaws, when I see them swallowing the meat and regurgitating it for the pups in the den, and the little ones greedily devouring everything, I know that everything makes sense. The 'blood-thirsty killer' is a devoted father.

But can wolves really kill every animal that they attack? Far from it! In general, about eighty per cent of attacks are unsuccessful, and the wolves go hungry. In times when food is in short supply, they can feed for a long time on mice, voles or beavers. Also, wolves aren't pure carnivores like cats; in the course of their evolution they drastically adapted their nutrition to their habitat, and to a great variety of sources of food. They became 'selective carnivorous omnivores'. That means that apart from their preferred prey, the large ungulates, they will also eat carrion, fish, vegetables and fruit. Some wolves have specialized in particular food sources, such as the wolves in the Great Bear Rainforest on the west coast of Canada. They catch salmon, but eat almost only the heads. Biologists attach two reasons to this preference: the brain and eye tissue of the fish contain high concentrations of docoshexaenoic acid (DHA), which is particularly important for the working of the nervous system. But the love of salmon heads could be a behaviour acquired through evolution, which protects the wolves against parasites. Some of the salmon are infected with bacteria, which can be deadly poisonous to Canidae. These bacteria are particularly concentrated in the muscle fabric and less in the heads of the fish.

Other wolves like pumpkins. In Spain, during the harvest of the vegetable, wolves drive the farmers to despair because they take just one bite out of almost every pumpkin.

And of course as real opportunists they grab anything that they can kill without effort – and that includes unguarded sheep and calves.

Wolves are not, in fact, equipped to attack large prey animals. Astonishing, isn't it, given that they are seen as the epitome of the effective hunter? Why, in spite of all their cooperation and team work, are they so unsuccessful at hunting? Why do most of their attacks fail?

In the killing of large prey animals there are several factors that make hunting difficult. Unlike big cats, wolves do not have a killing bite. Their long muzzles reduce the power of their biting muscles, and their canines and incisors wear down with age. They don't have retractable claws or powerful muscles in their front legs with which they can hold on to their prey, like pumas or grizzlies. Wolves only have feet for running and jaws for biting. The safest thing for them is to exhaust their prey by hounding, snapping and causing loss of blood, before they seriously attack. On every hunt the wolves work together. Every individual character type assumes its particular role, based on age, sex and social status. The best hunters in a wolf pack are two to three years old. And among wolves of the same age the smaller ones are generally worse hunters than the large ones, because more body mass is required for the killing of a significantly larger animal. Packs have the advantage when it comes to taking down prey, while the females are faster and better at hounding.

One other important factor in hunting is the size of the pack.

Wolves in groups of more than four tend to hold back when pursuing elk. Hunting success fails to increase with larger groups. Studies show that carnivore-hunting success peaks at two to five hunters, then levels off, or even declines, across larger group sizes. When hunting elk, that doesn't make any difference, but when hunting bison the number of wolves is just as crucial as cooperation within the pack.

Where hunting is concerned, wolves go on practising throughout their lives. They observe the parents and the other family members, and learn through experiment and very often through defeat.

Almost half of all prey killings occur in so-called 'environmental traps'. For example, if an elk cow escapes into a river, with her usual tactic, and the water is too shallow, she has miscalculated. If wolves are nearby, elk often move to more elevated areas, where it will be more difficult for the attackers to hunt them. Sometimes the wapitis will also run to a road that the predators avoid because of the presence of human beings. But this tactic can also develop into an environmental trap, because the wolves are very skilled at exploiting this situation. So they will deliberately chase the elk to a road where tourists are standing with their cars and encircle their prey. At such moments wolves can take down a wapiti in front of tourists and photographers.

Eat and be eaten.

Hunters and hunted have to find ways of surviving. That includes constantly rethinking plans and changing or adapting the parts that don't work.

If the killing of elk is dangerous for wolves, this is even more true of attacks on a bison weighing a tonne. They are the most difficult prey animals to kill, even more difficult than moose or musk oxen. Hunting bison requires not only physical power but mental strength. These are attributes associated with the Mollie wolf family. Whenever they appear, they remind me of the old western films, when the Indians appear lined up on their horses on the mountain crest. In its best times the pack consisted of twenty very large black wolves, which charged in closed formation at any unfortunate wolves who had ventured too far into their rivals' territory.

For a long time the Mollies tried to regain hold of Lamar Valley, their old hunting ground, from which they had once been expelled. Other wolf families there had occupied all the territories where there was sufficient prey. So they moved to Pelican Valley. In spring and summer this high valley in the inaccessible interior of the national park with nutritious grass is a true paradise for elk and bison. There is enough prey for wolves and grizzlies, and no roads for far and wide, and hence no disturbance by tourists. In the winter, however, the climate is the toughest on the whole continent, with icy temperatures, storms and deep snow. That's why in autumn both the elk and the bison mothers move down into Lamar Valley with their offspring. Left behind are smaller groups of bison bulls, which are robust enough to survive the pitiless weather. Some of them are old and tough, enormous muscular hulks, who manage to live on the sparse areas of grass revealed by the warmth of the hot springs. To save energy and store body fat the bison move very little.

For a wolf, even a weak bison is an enormous challenge. It took the Mollies several winters in the Pelican Valley to learn to deal with it, forced by the same tough conditions to become perfect bison hunters. Their technique is exceptional and reveals high intelligence. If bison are attacked, they don't run away; they stay where they are. Wolves hate that, because it makes the prey animals considerably better at defending themselves. The bison turn their massive heads towards their attackers. If the wolf comes from the side, they can turn in a flash. Direct attack is almost impossible, since the animals defend themselves as a group. They only become vulnerable if they walk in a row through deep snow.

For the bison, the wolves must use their complete environment to their advantage. To eat, the bison retreat to hills that are swept clear by the wind or thawed by the warmth of the earth. Here they are safe. If there are wolves nearby, they stop on these snow-free elevations and barely move to save valuable energy. If there are no predators nearby, they risk small excursions. The snow collects among the hills and makes it hard for the bison to defend themselves. Those are the spots where the wolves can attack.

The Mollies kill one of the big herbivores in the Pelican Valley every five to seven days. The leading biologist on the wolf project, Doug Smith, filmed one such attack by eight wolves on a bison, which, before it was brought down, killed a 55-kilo ten-month-old female wolf and caught two more on its horns and sent them flying through the air in a high arc. The female pack leader was also injured in the operation, and limped badly afterwards.

Only extremely hardened wolves can survive such passionate battles with bison. When the biologists captured some of the Mollies to fit them with radio collars, they included two yearlings, each of which already weighed almost 70 kilos.

The biologist Dan MacNulty filmed a spectacular battle by fourteen Mollie wolves against a single bison bull. Again and again the wolves drove the bison into deeper snow, jumped on its back and tore out great pieces of flesh. The bison shook the wolves off and threw its head back and forth to catch its attackers on its horns where possible. Wolves and bison became weaker and weaker in the course of the battle, which lasted for hours. But the wolves wouldn't give up. The bison lost in the end.

★

Human beings may once have observed the strategy of wolves in driving prey in a difficult environment. At some point early man noticed that they were similar to wolves. Both were carnivores, hunted in organized groups and shared their work. At the time they had almost the same body weight, and often preferred the large herbivores as prey. Only thanks to a sophisticated strategy and after a brief and intense effort can both wolves and humans kill prey animals that run faster or are stronger than themselves.

Although there is no genetic kinship between wolf and human, wolves give us remarkable clues as to how early hunting communities might have lived. They once hunted, ate and socialized, organized themselves and performed rituals in a similar way. And even today we live in the same ecosystem and have a similar ecological balance to maintain. Hence science today assumes a co-evolution of man and wolf.

The Mollies are a perfect example of how to make the best out of a bad situation with a new strategy and a successful plan. All the suitable territories were occupied. Did they throw up their paws and lament and wail about the injustice of the world? They had only two possibilities: to wage territorial wars with the other wolf packs and thus risk injury to their own families, or to seek alternative prey and a new hunting ground. Which is what they did. The market niche they found is not easy, and it is dangerous, but it made them the strongest and most feared wolf pack in Yellowstone.

If you observe wolves, you must be prepared for surprises, some of which wouldn't be out of place in the screenplay of a thriller. In April 2006 something happened that would make even the most experienced biologists shake their heads. For the first time in the history of wolf research I was able to witness the siege of a natal den by an unidentified wolf family.

The due date of the three pregnant females of the twelve Slough wolves was approaching. They were staying near the dens when twelve unfamiliar wolves invaded their territory. They too had a pregnant wolf in their midst. Over the next few days the interlopers stayed near the Slough dens all the time. At first the rightful owners retreated and merely engaged in howling competitions with the newcomers. Then a big Slough wolf was found dead and his pregnant partner disappeared. Meanwhile, the two other Slough wolves (one of them the alpha female) had moved into the natal den together to have their pups. Perhaps in view of the threat of danger shared shelter provided greater security and was easier to defend than two separate dens.

The siege began on the night of 12 April 2006. When I reached my observation point in the morning I saw nine of the besieging forces resting around the Slough den. At some point in the night they must have taken over the territory. They all seemed to be very interested in the natal den. One after another they poked their heads in but then jumped quickly back. From the radio signals we could tell that apart from the two wolf mothers and their newborn pups there was another female in the den.

The situation was life-threatening for the female wolves: suckling Canidae need a lot of fluid. If the mothers were trapped in the den, they could only survive for a short time.

The pregnant wolf from the rival pack tried to force her way several times into the Slough den, but was repeatedly forced back by snapping from inside.

The alien group besieged the natal den for thirteen days. Since without food the mothers didn't have enough milk for their young, the pups didn't survive. The small amount of food that a yearling could bring to the den every now and then wasn't enough for all of them.

In the end the Slough alpha male and another wolf that had

lingered near the den gave up and moved back to Lamar Valley. Meanwhile, the pregnant wolf from the besieging pack crept into another of the Slough dens and had her young on 24 April.

The next day the Slough mothers managed to leave the den unnoticed and return to their family. With them – but without pups – they headed west.

During the night of 26 April the situation worsened dramatically. The Sloughs returned, and there was a battle with the original besiegers, in the course of which one Slough wolf died and the alpha male was seriously injured; he died a short time later.

But the interlopers had paid their price as well. When they left the Slough territory a few weeks later, they did it without pups. Whether the Slough pups were killed, or whether they failed to survive because of the stress suffered by their mothers remains speculation.

These were scenes that could come from a handbook for psychological warfare. I don't know where the invaders came from and where they went. They were doubtless looking for a new home for their family. In this story there were no winners, only losers.

We humans can also sometimes get stuck and fail to see a way out. And sometimes we have to seek new niches so that we can be successful. At first glance these can be quite uncomfortable. Perhaps we may even need to develop completely new skills.

It's fundamentally important to develop a strategy for dealing with this situation. For that it is necessary to know where we stand exactly, not where we would like to stand; it's important to recognize where we are at this moment. Only then can we plan how to escape the situation and address the matter.

The Right Moment

Why Waiting Sometimes Brings Us Forward

Never give up. I couldn't help thinking of what my mother taught me as a child when, later in life, I observed the six wolves that had gathered on the riverbank. An elk cow stood in the water in front of them, her flanks quivering. She had escaped from her attackers into the river, where she was at an advantage with her long legs. To take her down, the wolves would have to swim to her, which was too dangerous, given that she could have kicked out at them with her front hooves. Now the pack distributed itself along both banks, lay down and waited. Success and failure are part of everyday life in the wolf world. Knowing when to take a risk, or when it's better to sit something out is an important ability of experienced pack leaders.

I recently watched a wolf pack driving a powerful bull elk to the edge of a cliff. They stared intensely at one another, like rivals before a boxing match. If the wolves were to attack, they would have fallen twenty metres into the abyss with their prey. After long consideration they gave up. The possibility of success wasn't worth the risk. They ran back into the forest, while the bull continued to stand on the cliff edge.

The cow in the river wasn't so lucky. Every time she tried to climb on to the shore, the attackers drove her back into the ice-cold water. The wolves knew her efforts were wasted. Six hours later they were able to kill their exhausted prey.

We too constantly have to make decisions in everyday life. Anyone with any intelligence knows that there is no point plunging blindly into a risky situation. At such moments you need to pause. The strength of wolves lies in their ability to gauge a situation and then decide how to proceed. Sometimes it's better to practise patience first of all, to think the situation through and weigh up your options. And sometimes, as with the wolves on the cliff, you have to admit that it makes no sense to take the next step. Then you just have to pull yourself together and start again.

That was how I felt when I gave up my legal career in favour of wolves. With great enthusiasm and the crazed hope of helping justice to victory, I had studied law and become an attorney. The reality of the first three years in the profession almost drove me to me despair. Divorces, traffic offences and crimes. Bureaucracy and frustration. It wasn't how I'd imagined it. I took stock and wondered whether I really wanted to practise this profession for the rest of my life. After all, it was my precious lifetime. I wanted to get off the treadmill, but I didn't want to act unthinkingly and over-hastily. So I came up with a plan. I calculated my finances and looked for possible ways of spending a long time getting by with alternative jobs while at the same time making my dream come true: I wanted to do something with wolves. When the opportunity came up to do an internship in behavioural research in a wolf research facility in the USA, I grabbed it. That was when my wolfish life began. I'm often asked if I've ever regretted it. Never! The wolves have taught me not to look back. I was unhappy as a lawyer, and for that reason not good enough at my job. The logical consequence for me was to take the next step. For me it was the best decision of my life.

It's important to bear in mind that decisions don't always need to be taken straight away. Sometimes, when a situation looks hopeless, it can be useful to hold out for a while and wait for the right moment. I was taught that by a little gopher with a desperate desire for survival.

I watched a young wolf carrying a living gopher in her mouth. She set the animal down on the ground and started playing with it like a cat with a mouse. She showed her teeth and snarled at it, stamped her foot near her prey, lay down right beside it and growled. The brave gopher didn't move. At last it stirred, stood on its hind legs, bared two big gopher teeth and prodded its little front foot at the wolf. It looked as if it were trying to box. This 'fight' between the unmatched species lasted almost ten minutes. When another yearling distracted the wolf, the gopher took the opportunity and ran for cover.

Persistence and patience are two qualities that I often envy wolves, particularly when I'm in yet another traffic jam. Patience isn't a strength of mine. I want everything immediately. But in Yellowstone I learned to redefine the concept of time. Nature isn't interested in how much of a hurry we're in. It has its own rhythm.

For many years I worked as a guide in Yellowstone, showing the wolves to German animal-lovers. They saw the places where the predators most liked to linger, they got to know the characteristics of the individual wolf personalities and the structures of the wolf families, and received tips on what to notice when observing animals.

In a preparatory conversation, someone would usually ask: 'What do I need for the tour?' They meant equipment, but that's of secondary importance, because I supply the kit. The most important quality that anyone who wants to investigate wild animals needs to bring along is patience. Being able to wait. The will to observe sleeping wolves for hours at a time. While some of the bipeds get bored after only half an hour, we hardcore wolf-observers quickly learned our lesson from the quadrupeds and if necessary waited for four hours at minus 30 degrees until the wolves woke up.

In today's rapid-paced digital age it is pleasantly calming to observe wild animals. They seem to have all the time in the world. Let us take the scene of a dead elk that the wolves have killed: a grizzly has taken possession of the carcass and driven the competition away. In a typically bear-like way, it piled grass and dirt on its prey, lay down in the middle of it and enjoyed its post-prandial nap. Five wolves have rolled up around the bear and gone to sleep. In the trees there are a few bald eagles yearningly eyeing the food. They all wait patiently until the bear wakes up and leaves. They wait, and eventually the prey will be theirs.

Nature has a time of its own. You notice that particularly in long-term observations. We can't measure such things by human standards. When the first wolves came back to Yellowstone in 1995, after an absence of seventy years, we still had no idea what effect they would have on their prey animals and the ecosystem as a whole. We would only understand that later on. Even today, that development hasn't yet finished, and probably never will. Nature has taught me to live on a different timescale. What are two or three years of our life compared to the life of a grizzly (thirty years) or a ten-thousand-year-old river? You experience the time of trees differently when you're surrounded by them. I am always struck by the patience of trees when I look at an old oak. Knowing that such a tree spends 300 years growing, 300 years living and 300 years dying, my way of thinking changed. The world thinks and lives in different timescales, and doesn't give a damn about me. That's enormously liberating.

There was once a ketchup advertisement in the USA, in which it seemed to take forever for the long-awaited red blob to land on the hamburger. The slogan 'The best things come to those who wait' also applies to wolves. Unless they get lucky and are in the right place at the right time.

For several days in May 2011 I watched a one-year-old female wolf from the Lamar pack trying in vain to hunt pronghorns. I felt sorry for her, because these antelope-like animals are among the fastest land-based animals on earth. They can run up to 70 kilometres an hour, and they're also extremely alert. No chance for the young, inexperienced wolf – I thought. She always hunted alone, and the other wolves seemed to take no interest in her 'pointless' undertaking. I myself had quietly made fun of her: when's she finally going to work out that she can't catch antelopes? But then one of the pronghorns stepped in a hole in the snow and stumbled. The wolf shot over, grabbed its prey by the ankle and held it long enough for the other wolves to arrive and take down the animal together. Now I had to ask forgiveness. Eventually, all that practice had paid off. Even today she likes hunting pronghorns. Perhaps she likes the challenge. But perhaps she just wants to try something out. And once again the wolves made something clear to me: the longer I observe them, the less I know about them.

Unlike many people, wolves don't always immediately connect everything with achievement. For us it may be humiliating if we can't do something straight away. We think we can't afford to make mistakes, and we allow ourselves to be distracted, and often frustrated, by thoughts of achievement and comparison. At the same time we often forget how appealing it can be to learn something new. But to do that we need to cultivate the art of patience. The essence of patience lies in accepting the natural rhythm of life and not trying to adapt it to our human timetable.

The Game of Life

Why We Should Never Stop Playing

Lamar Valley, Yellowstone National Park: the Lamar wolves are having a siesta in the February sun. When they wake up, the little wolf family is almost bursting with energy. They all leap up, lick each other's muzzles, jump over one another, throw themselves on their backs and catapult the others into the air with their paws. Peace only returns slowly. But two wolves haven't yet had enough. They play at hunting and catching and have finally discovered that sliding down the hill is terrific fun. They run up the mountain and slide back down on the snow. Again and again. They look like over-excited children.

Switch of scene: Banff National Park. Yukon is a two-year-old adult wolf. But he still behaves like an adolescent. He kicks soft-drink cans around in front of him like a football player, before finally 'scoring' with them. And he does that again and again too.

Why do wolves do that? There is no rational explanation. The Lamar wolves are perfectly healthy. They have no skin diseases that might make them itchy and restless. And Yukon, as an experienced hunter, doesn't need to improve his motor skills for the catching of prey. No, the wolves are plainly just having fun.

What – fun? Aren't fun and joy the exclusive privilege of human beings? Animals don't have emotions. Their whole behaviour is either instinct or survival training. At least that's what we've learned, and that's what it says in a number of books. But the reality looks different.

'Anyone who works a lot is also allowed to play a lot!' Wolves seem to live according to this saying. Nonetheless, play for them is more than just fun. It is a form of social learning. Wolfish play occurs on a higher social level, and is always accompanied by a feeling of well-being through the release of dopamine.

Adult wolves play chase, tug of war or hide-and-seek. They bring each other little gifts, usually small pieces of food or bones, and strut provocatively up and down in front of the others until they chase them. And old wolves playing with pups look as if they have fallen into a fountain of youth.

The Lamar wolves infect their drowsy parents with their playfulness. They join in with a joyful game of sliding, until the fun threatens to overflow because the uninhibited young ones are taking it too far. The adults impose peace again by standing in the way of the young hotheads, reining in their enthusiasm and bringing the boisterous game to an end. The young wolves fall into the snow with a deep snort and within a very short time they are fast asleep.

Play is a practical method of communicating with one another, a good physical workout and a strengthening of social bonds. The wolves who play with each other most are the ones who are already friends, and who also lie closely together when they sleep. The same is true of human beings.

Play is a time for learning and training in which everyone gathers experiences to help their fellows. But it's also a way of interacting on a high ethical and moral level, in which social roles are taught or reversed and fair play is practised. When

animals play with one another, there are agreements that must be kept. The 'golden rule' seems to exist even among wolves. 'Do as you would be done by.' Following this principle requires empathy and the will to set aside differences (physical size, social rank) for the duration of the game. Anyone who doesn't want to play along is avoided by the others, spends more time alone and, for that reason, may leave the family earlier and try to make it on their own. However, life outside the social group is significantly riskier than within the security of the family. The biologist Marc Bekoff holds the view that in social species natural selection excludes cheats, those who do not play according to negotiated and accepted rules. Animals, like human beings, survive and flourish better when they play fair and learn the moral code for behaviour in their group. So presumably Darwin was right when he speculated that empathetic animals reproduce more successfully and are therefore better at survival.

Through play wolf pups learn fairness, cooperation and what

is allowed and what isn't. They learn that there is a chance of being injured if they don't stick to the rules, and that their fellow will lose interest in playing if they are too rough and reckless. One important feature of play is self-control. Young animals, for example, learn through play how hard they can bite. Adult wolves can develop a biting force of 150 kilonewtons, or up to 1.5 tonnes per square centimetre. That is twice the biting force of a normal dog, reason enough to hold back that power.

One important criterion for play is the readiness of adults, and particularly of high-ranking adults, to slip into the role of the 'underdog' and voluntarily be thrown on their backs. This is an example of role reversal. You remember Druid pack leader 21? At the ripe old age of eight he loved his peace, but still liked playing with his son and would let him win. The yearling pulled him by his ruff, kicked his legs out from under him and threw him on the ground. Then he stood assertively over his dad, who would then free himself, before allowing himself to be thrown on the ground again a short time later. That way the young wolf learned what it's like to fight against a big, stronger wolf and defeat them.

Through self-control and role reversal wolves learn what behaviour towards another animal is acceptable, and how to resolve conflicts. That is also one of the reasons why human children should be encouraged to participate in team sports, and why parents shouldn't mind letting their kids win at games.

One very popular game with the Yellowstone wolves is to break the ice on a lake or a river. The wolves stand on a freshly frozen lake and jump up and down on the ice with their front paws until it cracks. Or they slide together across the frozen surface, in something like a mixture of figure skating and dodgem cars. A group of young wolves run on to the ice, crash into each other, jostle one another, jump over each other and slide on until they have their paws under control again.

The whole family also seems to enjoy games of hide-and-seek. One of them will hide in a dip or behind a hill. He will peer carefully out to see what his fellow player is doing, and immediately duck back down again. The other one searches (or pretends to search), and as soon as he nears the one who is hiding, he jumps out and 'scares' him. Then they begin a wild game of chase.

Anything at all can be a toy. From a stick, old bones and scraps of fur to a poor mouse that is in the wrong place at the wrong time. But the wolves are particularly interested in objects that humans have left behind, such as T-shirts or baseball caps. When road repairs were being done, the workmen left behind some of their orange plastic cones, which were enthusiastically carried off by a group of young wolves. They dragged them off, jumped on them, threw them into the air and finally shredded them into small, manageable pieces.

But wolves can also keep themselves entertained. One winter I observed a female wolf who must have got bored. She started plucking pine cones from the tree. She got up on her hind legs and stretched high enough to pull down the cones, which she then threw in the air like ping-pong balls, then either caught them or let them roll down the slope before sliding after them. Necessity (to play) is the mother of invention.

Every game requires a decent portion of curiosity. For wolves the world is a source of constant surprise. They take nothing for granted, but prefer to get to the bottom of everything. Every situation promises miracles, discoveries and surprises as far as they are concerned. In this they're like human children.

The American wolf biologist L. Dave Mech spent many years with a pack of Arctic wolves on Ellesmere Island in the Arctic. The animals, who had quickly got used to him, observed all his movements, and kept stealing underwear, his sleeping bag or other objects out of his tent to examine them in depth – and then to roll around on them.

The wolf researcher Günther Bloch had similar experiences. The favourite occupation of the Bow Valley wolf pack that he observed in Banff National Park was to steal and destroy camping equipment. The wolves were raising their pups in a den only 150 metres from a campsite. At least three times a week a young female wolf, who was the babysitter for the little ones, would march straight to the campsite, steal a baseball, a pillow or a backpack from the tourists and carry the objects to the den. The pups loved their new toys. Together, they examined them and took them apart. After a while the area around the den looked like a battlefield.

This habit became a kind of family occupation. All the pups played with some kind of waste product of civilization, and tried to tug a soft-drink can or a piece of rucksack away from each other. The wolf parents also took part in this frenzy of destruction. For weeks the wolves stayed near the campers. Even in the autumn, when the young wolves were bigger, the wolf family came back several times to their special adventure playground. Again they deliberately looked for objects that they could tear apart. One day there was a car tyre by a tree. A tourist must have left it there. The wolves weren't at all interested in the nearby four-by-four. They immediately ran to the tyre and sniffed at it briefly. Then a black wolf grabbed it and tried to shake it like a prey animal. That was the starting signal for the rest of the family. All of a sudden they worked as one, and the wolves were soon ripping pieces out of it. In less than half an hour the scraps were scattered all around the landscape.

Sometimes I wonder whether children these days actually know how to play with each other. If they spend their time looking at iPhones or iPads, the social activities so important for children's development don't take place. And what about playing among adults? Do we know how to do that? We're so preoccupied with our everyday routine that we often don't even have time to play in the family. There always seems to be something more important to do. So – who has the right idea about the significance of play, wolves or humans?

When Bad Things Happen to Good Wolves

Overcoming Fears of Loss and Surviving Bad Times

When the alarm clock rang in my cabin in Silver Gate at five o'clock in the morning, I was already awake, and had had my third cup of coffee. It was still too dark to drive in the park. I had barely slept that night. I uneasily prepared my picnic for my wolf-watching session, made some cheese on toast, packed a few carrots and apples, and made a pot of tea. My thoughts kept returning to the previous day when Cinderella, the alpha female of the Druid pack, had gone missing.

I had watched her that day near the frozen Slough Creek on the western rim of Lamar Valley. She and her family had spent several hours lying lazily in the afternoon sun. She was big for a female wolf, almost 50 kilos, and as with her companion her black fur was turning grey with age.

I got a warm feeling in my heart when I saw the pair lying snugly together licking each other's muzzles. They had been inseparable for many years.

The other members of the Druid wolf family – eight adults and nine yearlings – were dozing nearby, some of them rolled up in tight balls, their tails wrapped round their bodies.

Cinderella's thick winter coat shone in the sun. She had never looked more beautiful. The intimacy of the two wolves was impressive. Even though she was a strong and independent character, her partner seemed to want to protect her.

I continued my observation round through the valley. On the way back I wanted to take a look at the Druids, but they had disappeared. I drove home. In the evening I called my friends from the wolf project and learned that the pack had come back without Cinderella. 'They looked for her and howled.'

Something was wrong. Over the many years I have spent with wolves, I have developed a kind of sixth sense, a feeling in my gut that tells me when something is wrong. I got very worried and brooded all night about what might have happened.

When the sun began to rise the next morning behind the Absaroka mountains, I drove into the park. At Slough Creek I could see the car belonging to Carol and Richard from Oregon who, like me, come several times a year to see the wolves. Cinderella is their favourite wolf too.

They both greeted me with anxious expressions.

'So?' I asked Richard.

'Nothing!'

A chorus of howling gave us a start and a wolf appeared on the mountain.

He was greyish-black with a dark strip on his nose. Cinderella's partner, the Druid alpha, sat up and threw back his head in a long lament. His hot breath froze on contact with the air and left little ice crystals on his nose.

A mile further south-west, two wolves were howling excitedly from the 3,000-metre-high tip of Specimen Ridge. Another group answered their calls, their voices coming from Tower Junction, near Yellowstone River.

So much howling was unusual. It must have been three packs. The usual territorial racket in the mating season sounds different. This was more intense. Now I was sure that something had happened.

We waited impatiently for Rick McIntyre, the biologist with the telemetric equipment. When his yellow Suzuki pulled into the lay-by beside us, we could tell by his serious expression that it was better not to talk to him. He walked a little way along the road, turned the hand antenna in all directions and listened to the beeps from the receiver, which were getting louder and louder. The Druids were in foreign territory. Meanwhile, the alpha male was howling uninterruptedly, and there was not a sign of Cinderella.

'That's never happened before. She's always with the pack,' Rick said, then climbed into his car and drove away to check the radio signals from different positions.

'I hope she's OK,' Carol said quietly.

Rick told us over the walkie-talkie that he had received a faint signal from Cinderella from Specimen Ridge. That was the territory of the Mollies, their deadly rivals. This wolf family and the Druids had been at war for many years over the excellent hunting territory in Lamar Valley. Sometimes one wolf group won, sometimes the other. At the moment the Druids ruled the valley, but the Mollies had recently tried repeatedly to win it back. And now that was where they were.

We heard the sound of an aeroplane engine, and a short time later saw the wolf biologists' one-propeller yellow Cessna circling over the mountain. They were looking for the missing wolf too. The plane has aerials on its fuselage, and can locate the frequencies of the radio collars from the air.

'They're trying to get signals from her,' Rick told us over the radio. What he didn't tell us was that he'd received a 'dead signal' from Cinderella's collar – an indication that the wolf hadn't moved for several hours. It doesn't necessarily mean anything bad. Sometimes the collar falls off or there's an error.

But this time there was no error. From the plane the scientists saw the blood-drenched body of the alpha female on the mountain peak. Later they told us: 'She died at one of the most beautiful spots in the park, with a view of Yellowstone River.'

Meanwhile, the workers on the wolf project had been informed about Cinderella's disappearance and had passed on the news. More and more wolf fans were turning up at the spot where the female wolf had last been seen. We gathered on a hill and observed the Druids. The sixteen wolves were dozing in the afternoon sun. The atmosphere was gloomy and unusually quiet. In our thoughts, many of us were with the wolf family on the mountain.

When Rick joined us, he had tears in his eyes. In a soft, quiet voice he told us that Cinderella had been killed. 'We're still trying to reconstruct everything, but we assume it must have been the Mollies.'

Carol sobbed. 'I'm glad we were here when it happened,' Richard said. 'At least she wasn't shot.'

At that moment 21, the Druid alpha, got to his feet, sat down on the snow and howled. His lament filled the valley and moved us all deeply. We were suffering with him.

The next day the grieving wolf ran into the den area where Cinderella had raised their pups over the last few years. His howling could be heard for three more days. Then he mated with another female from his pack. Life went on.

Only six months later Wolf 21 disappeared as well. Months later his skeleton was found in an area where he had spent many months with his partner. The cause of death remained unclear. Perhaps he had died of old age, or perhaps he was severely injured in the attempt to kill an elk. After his disappearance there was great confusion in the wolf family. Within a few months the wolves had lost both parents. Again they howled for a long time and searched – until again life resumed its course and a new pair of pack leaders was found.

Pain and grief, but also joy and responsibility. For a long time scientific researchers believed that only human beings were capable of such emotions. Meanwhile, people's thinking has changed. Cognitive ethology investigates the learning, memory, thoughts, sensations and emotions of animals. This also involves the ability to project our own ideas and experiences on to other living creatures. Decision-making. Insight. Foresight, spatial orientation, anticipatory behaviour and other qualities previously attributed only to human beings have now been identified in all living creatures. And yet the existence of emotions in animals is still not universally accepted.

One example from Canada, related to me by my fellow researcher Günther Bloch, shows that wolves don't only grieve, but can even die of heartache. Betty and Stoney were the parents of the Cascade wolf family in Banff National Park. For eight years they led a pack of eighteen animals, and the calm self control with which they responded to the other animals was very striking. One autumn, Betty was found dead near the body of an elk bull. She was just skin and bone. It was impossible to establish how she had died. Laboratory studies revealed that her immune system had been seriously weakened and she had suffered several broken ribs, although most of them had quickly healed. With the death of the female pack leader a dynasty came to an end. About two weeks later they also found the dead alpha male, Stoney. He lay rolled up in a dip just a few kilometres from the place of Betty's death. A thorough investigation in the laboratory did not reveal any notable injuries. Unlike his companion, Stoney had been in good physical shape. The cause of his death remained a mystery: how had this strong male wolf died? The Canadian biologist Paul C. Paquet had a surprising explanation: a 'broken heart'. In all likelihood, Stoney's close relationship with his partner led to his death. After the companion with whom he had lived closely for over eight years and raised a number of pups had died the lonely old man simply didn't want to go on living.

Can we still dispute, after examples like this, that highly developed, social creatures feel emotions such as love, concern or fidelity? It's time to think in new categories.

Animals miss their companions too, when they pass away. As long as they live, they have a close bond and look after one another. If one of them goes away, the other one looks for them. We don't need to understand grief to feel it. We grieve when a beloved human or a beloved animal dies, because we miss them. And eventually we adapt and carry on.

When wolves are killed by their own kind, it's painful for me as an observer, but it's a natural process of life. It was different when She-Wolf was shot.

In the spring of 2012 the American government took wolves off the endangered species list, and hunting was permitted in Montana and Wyoming. On 6 December 2012 hunters outside Yellowstone shot the charismatic female leader of the Lamar pack. They had lured her out of the protected Yellowstone National Park with bait. As I have mentioned before, there was a furious outcry from the wolf community. Fans of She-Wolf from all over the world protested and demanded a ban on hunting on the edges of the park.

From the moment the government took wolves off the list, I feared that news. I had hoped that the hunters wouldn't kill wolves with collars, since they knew that these animals were part of a scientific research programme. But I had underestimated the hatred of the enemies of wolves. Of the twelve park wolves shot that winter, six were wearing collars. Hunters had spread the frequencies of the radio collars on the internet, so that they could deliberately kill these wolves. To make it even more painful, they posted messages on social media, like 'Wolves make brilliant bedroom rugs'. They didn't just want to destroy the hated animals, they wanted to hurt all wolf fans. And it didn't stop. Again and again there were new reports of wolves being shot or killed in steel traps. It was as if a terrible spirit had been released from a bottle.

Wolves leave no one untouched. Those of us who love them try with all our might to protect them. But hatred and passionate desire to kill them are often stronger.

How do we deal with the bad things that happen to us and the people we love? Until then I had lived in an idyllic world. Of course, like all of us, I had suffered losses. Humans and animals I had loved had died. But never before had I been confronted by such open hatred.

Everyone who works with wolves knows about conflict with the opponents of wolves. It's part of our lives and part of our work. I could live with that. But someone killing innocent animals for fun and to hurt other human beings, that was too much for me. I had no idea how much it would throw me off course.

When I learned in Germany of the death of my favourite female wolf, I was shattered. I had accompanied She-Wolf for many years. She had grown close to my heart with her impressive personality.

How was I to deal with it? I didn't want to see any more wolves dying. I didn't want to feel that powerlessness any more, that deep fury towards the hunters. I withdrew, and for a while I didn't even read the email reports that friends from the wolf project sent me every day, for fear of fresh bad news. My usual strategies for dealing with loss had ceased to function.

I felt like the wolf mother whose companion for many years had died at the age of twelve. She left her territory and her nine-month-old pups with her family. The female wolf moved many kilometres westwards into inaccessible territory and couldn't be located. Then, one day, she was back. Presumably she had used that time to grieve.

In the old days, when I lost someone close to me, I escaped to Yellowstone immediately afterwards. The wilderness helped me to heal. It's a place that offers comfort, a place of wonders and humility, where I am at one with everything and never alone. But this time I couldn't escape to Yellowstone, because my wilderness there was no longer idyllic. It was a place of suffering, disasters and death. There were hunters. I wanted to get away from everything, but I couldn't run away from the pain.

Why did the death of a wild wolf, whom I had only observed from a distance, touch me so much?

Like all of those who observe wild animals over a long period of time, we establish a bond with them. We are granted an intimate glance into their lives and get to know them. It's like a loving relationship. Sometimes when we form a particularly deep relationship, we recognize ourselves in the other party. That's how it was for me with She-Wolf. I recognized myself in the independent wolf. The loss hit me all the harder. Not her death as such, but the cowardly, underhand way she had had to die.

All of a sudden I was confronted by questions for which I had no answers. Questions about the meaning of life. For decades I had taught people about wolves, confident that people protect what they know. Had it all been in vain? Did what I do have any influence at all? Did it make a difference? Or did nothing matter anyway?

After grief over the loss of She-Wolf came fury. But fury isn't a solution, and neither is it something that you should carry around with you for a long time. Suddenly I was afraid of going back to Yellowstone. Afraid of getting too attached to the wolves, only to lose them again. She-Wolf's death hadn't just torn the Lamar wolf family apart, it had left me completely distraught. Would the fury ever fade?

I remembered an event that had happened a few years ago in New York. A young woman had been brutally raped and beaten by six men. The perpetrators left her lying there, because they thought she was dead. She survived and later said in the trial that she forgave the perpetrators. She said to the astonished judge that the men had done something terrible to her and robbed her of a valuable part of her life. She didn't want to give them the power to take more of her life away by staying angry with them. She forgave them to be free again.

When my fury with the hunters threatened to overwhelm me I thought about this remarkable statement which I've never forgotten. Did I want to make the rest of my life and my serenity dependent on the actions of other people? It was time to bear in mind the wisdom of the wolves.

What do they do when bad things happen to them? Do they lament and grieve? Yes! Do they die of loneliness and longing for their dead partner? Some of them do. Do they doubt the meaning of their life? No!

I slowly found peace with that thought. She-Wolf had always been a fighter. She would never have given up. She would go on hunting, living, loving, just as I had to go on. I would keep on observing wolves and telling their stories. And perhaps that way I would one day help to end the killing.

When I came back to Yellowstone after a year-long break, I was still mourning She-Wolf's death. I sensed her presence everywhere. But it helped me concentrate on nature and the other animals in the park: the bison, of which there were as many as ever this year. The coyotes that – in the absence of their big competitors – now had much more prey at their disposal. The otters, eagles and bighorn sheep helped me over the loss of my favourite wolf and showed me that life goes on.

One evening just before sunset I sat on a rock in Lamar Valley and scoured the landscape with my binoculars. In the distance I heard coyotes howling excitedly. A herd of bison moved past me, grazing peacefully. All of a sudden, behind me and at an angle, I heard something moving. I didn't stir, and waited. A greyish-brown female wolf trotted into my field of vision. She had her eye on a newborn bison calf, on which she was focusing all her attention. I struggled not to breathe, so as not to break the spell. About 3 metres in front of me she noticed me, stopped and looked at me. No, she seemed to look right through me as if I weren't interesting enough to bother about. The gaze of a wolf that passes through you and ignores you can wound and delight at the same time. Was I so insignificant that I wasn't even worth a hint of fear? Would she grin at me with mischievous glee if I looked at her wide-eyed and frozen with fear?

She simply didn't care that I was there. She wasn't bothered about whether I was afraid of her or wanted to hug her. I was only an insignificant part of her environment – not edible, and hence not important.

Then I remembered where I had seen the facial expression of that wolf before – on her mother. Two years ago I had stood with a few friends on a mountain, looking for wolves through the scope. 'Watch out, behind us,' someone had suddenly whispered. We turned cautiously round. And there stood She-Wolf. While we had been looking for her in the valley, she had walked around us in a wide arc, sized us up and decided that we weren't worth getting worked up about.

Now her daughter was clearly standing in front of me, and I recognized the same expression and the same way of reacting to human beings. And for the first time in ages peace and joy returned to my heart.

Wolves grieve. When a family member dies or disappears they go searching, they are unsettled and sometimes aggressive, they howl dolefully and for a long time. But eventually they pull themselves together, get up and get on with things. They follow the rhythm of life: they hunt, eat, reproduce and look after their families. They do what all living creatures do in nature: they celebrate the here and now. Only we humans seem to have lost this ability. We constantly worry about our future, or bury ourselves in the past. If only we could live more in the present! Animals teach us how. Let us step back and observe them. Let's be like they are, learn from them and grow with them. And let us understand that they move on when it's time for them to leave this world, and we are left behind, a little richer for having known them. Unfortunately we live in a world that has taught us to hang and cling on to everything. That way, time and again, we experience loss and an almost unbearable emptiness. I have learned a lot from the Yellowstone wolves. Above all, to accept those things that cannot be changed, to adapt and drink life down – each day anew.

Let's Just Save the World

The Secret of an Intact Ecosystem

One cold autumn morning just before sunrise I took a short drive into the valley of the wolves. One of the most beautiful seasons had begun. The mountain world of Wyoming and Montana exploded in an ecstasy of colour, with golden aspens and blood-red maple trees. The first snow powdered the mountain-tops and the hordes of tourists were in distinct decline. An overnight layer of hoar frost covered the backs of the bison, and the bald eagles could be seen circling in the air. In the more elevated areas the elks had started courting, and the bears were filling their bellies ahead of their long winter sleep.

For wolves autumn is one of the hardest times of the year. The little ones aren't yet fully fledged members of the hunting party, and thus a bit of a nuisance for the pack. The prey animals are strong and healthy. Now every wolf family has its paws full feeding its young. The bigger the pack, the harder this task is. At the same time it is getting too crowded in the families, so during this season a lot of sexually mature animals emigrate from their home territory.

I stopped in a lay-by and opened the car window in spite of the frost. It was rutting season for the big wapiti bulls. Their hoarse calls sound like a cross between a squeaking door and the braying of a donkey, and coming from the mouths of such imposing animals, it is so unusual that some tourists hearing it for the first time turn round curiously to look for where the strange noise is coming from. The rutting season is also when the bulls are at their most aggressive, and could even attack a car as a potential rival. The big wapiti are in a state of constant tension as they try to keep their ladies together and at the same time keep competitors away. Out of sheer stress they can barely tell whether their adversary is a wolf, a grizzly or a car, and at the end of the long mating season they are often so exhausted that they can barely stand up.

I saw something moving in the middle of the valley. Birds flew up and coyotes ran around. The wolves had had a successful hunt during the night and left an elk carcass behind. Now ravens, bald eagles and coyotes fought over the remains. It wouldn't be long before the first bears arrived and demanded their share. I climbed out of the car and set up my equipment. Even if the wolves weren't around, a carcass still provided interesting experiences and visual material demonstrating how nothing in nature is wasted.

Over the next few hours six coyotes, two bald eagles, a golden eagle and a grizzly bear met up at the groaning table. Countless ravens and magpies fought over the smaller scraps.

There are 450 different varieties of beetle in Yellowstone that live on carcasses, more than fifty of them directly dependent on the meat that the wolves supply for them. Many also eat other beetles. A whole predator–prey community lives like a microcosm on each carcass.

When, after a few days, weeks and months, nothing is left but bleached bones, the ground on the spot where the carcass lay will contain 100 to 600 per cent more inorganic nitrogen, phosphorus and potassium than the surrounding area. Some species, such as moose, like eating plants that are rich in nitrogen. The urine and faeces of these herbivores contribute even more to the fertility of the soil. More bacteria and fungi also grow on these spots.

How little we still know about connections in nature! It was only through years of observing wolves that I learned that it's not a matter of individual species, but that we are all part of a whole. Our ecosystem is a fine and sensitive network in which every plant and every living creature has its place – even us. If we take something out, the puzzle shifts. Wolves are a significant part of this ecosystem. When they were relocated to the national park, everything changed.

In Yellowstone, the ecological card game was reshuffled by the return of wolves, and new rules of play were established for the survival of many animal species. This produced effects that follow on from one another in a great torrent. Researchers call it the 'ecology of fear'.

So, for example, in the first two years wolves reduced the coyote population by half. They saw their small relatives as competitors for food and killed them. This led to an increase in the numbers of rodents, voles and gophers – the food of coyotes – which in turn became available to predators, such as foxes, hawks, owls, martens and badgers, leading to a growth in their numbers.

The grizzlies too quickly learned to appreciate the return of the wolves. They follow them and take their prey from them. Almost every carcass is very swiftly taken over by grizzlies. Because the wolves provide sufficient protein even in the winter months and the spring, more and more bears come out of hibernation early. After giving birth to their cubs they are hungry, and red meat is an incredibly rich source of nutrition and energy.

Some changes in the prey species are so amazing that you don't immediately make the connection: since the wolves came back, for example, the pronghorns moved their birth sites closer to the wolf dens. *Isn't that pure suicide?* you'll be wondering. On the contrary – here once again we have proof of how extremely adaptable and inventive wild animals are. The new-born pronghorn fawns are a favourite seasonal dish for coyotes. Hunting adult pronghorns uses up too much energy even for the nimble, swift coyotes. For that reason they have to kill the fawns before they're old enough to run away. The pronghorn mothers' only strategy is to hide their young in the bushes. But today we know that the areas with the highest survival rates for pronghorns are near wolf dens. Wolves rarely hunt the animals because they are too fast for them. But coyotes avoid the vicinity of wolves like the plague. So the clever herbivores have chosen to be near wolves as it is the safest place for their off-spring. Remarkable!

It is an undisputed fact that wolves have an effect on the other animals in Yellowstone National Park. But their influence on the landscape and trees is still scientifically controversial. For example, the state of the willows and poplars in the northern part of the park has been a contentious issue. The young trees and bushes near the shore are a favourite food of the wapiti. In the years before the return of the wolves most of the willows along the river didn't grow higher than a metre. The elk didn't give the fresh growth in the spring a chance. An absence of taller bushes means that there is no shade of the kind that trout or songbirds like.

Then the wolves were introduced, and the sated, contented life of the ungulates was at an end. It wasn't just that the predators reduced the population size of the wapiti; they also changed their eating habits. The elk lingered less often by the riverbank and instead stayed in the open valley, where they had a better view of their enemy. The shade cast by the willows led to cooler water, and the trout, more songbirds and, in the end, also the beavers came back. That was the 'wolf effect' – at least in theory.

It could have been so nice: the wolves rescue trees, beavers and fish. Hurray! Bring us wolves so that our planet may heal again! So is that Russian proverb true, the one that says 'Where the wolf hunts the forest grows'? Unfortunately it isn't as simple as that, because the ecosystem is distinctly more complex.

A study published in 2010 robbed us of the illusion of the wolf as a noble saviour. It suggested that elk simply aren't afraid enough of wolves to alter their feeding habits. Adult wapiti are hard for wolves to kill. Not only are they much bigger than their attackers, their hooves are also a danger to them. And they find protection in the herd, which notices approaching wolves more quickly than an individual animal.

But why did the landscape change in spite of all this? Now the beaver comes into play, an animal that has a key role in the growth of willows. Beavers need the trees for food and to build fortresses and dams, which hold back the water, which the willows need to grow. In the days before the return of the wolves elk ate so many willows that there were none left for the beavers and the big rodents disappeared. Without wolves and beavers the ecosystem changed so much that it was practically irreparable.

So it isn't the *behaviour* of elk as such that has an influence on the growth of the trees and the change to the landscape, but their *number*. However, wolves alone can't be held responsible for the decline in the elk population. Many other factors also play a role, such as climate change and the decades of drought that have affected the land. So, for example, grizzly bears that can't find enough food kill large numbers of elk calves. And then there's the yearly elk hunt on the fringes of the park, in which thousands of wapiti are slaughtered.

Scientists still argue over which species have the greatest effect on an ecosystem – the ones at the top of a food chain or the ones at the bottom. In order to understand nature as a whole, we need to look at the smallest creatures. The influence of other living things on the ecosystem is left out of the equation too often, even today. While specialists go on talking about whether elk or bison have more of a lasting impact on the landscape of Yellowstone, in some years masses of grasshoppers land on the park and eat twice as much as all the herbivores together. Hardly anyone thinks that's worth mentioning.

At the same time, science has imposed the view that nature tends to be governed more from top to bottom than the other way around. So the return of the wolves confirms that large predators have a significant effect on the structure and function of natural systems and change the whole ecosystem. Since wolves have resettled their old home, the spectrum of predators – grizzlies, black bears, mountain lions and wolves – is complete again after seventy years. However, the changes are clearly visible, but they are by no means complete.

It remains to be seen how the ecosystem will adapt again over the decades to come. It's impossible to make any predictions here, since there are too many unknown factors. It is nature's plan to ensure stability in the long term, while in the short term the ecosystem is extremely changeable. Climate change (hard winters, dry summers), forest fires, illnesses afflicting wolves and their prey animals – all of this can affect the ecosystem. As an extremely adaptable predator, which reacts very quickly to changing environmental conditions, the wolf can not only influence the ecosystem, but also stabilize it. But that takes time.

We still expect much too much, and too quickly. We expect that we'll be able to reintroduce a species into an ecosystem and a few years later everything will go according to plan. We don't factor in setbacks, the unpredictable. But nature constantly throws our lovely calculations into chaos. However much we might wish, there are no simple solutions or easy answers.

So do wolves make our ecosystem healthier? Yes, definitely,

but it's not enough. The wolf can't save within a few years what man has destroyed on a grand scale over millennia. Maintaining an intact ecosystem is so much easier than understanding it and repairing it after important pieces have been lost. That takes a huge amount of rethinking – and a miracle.

Anyone who walks through nature open-eyed can experience a miracle. Like many of us wolf fanatics I concentrated for a long time on the large predators, without seeing the mysteries of the fascinating smaller animals. That has changed. While I spend many hours in nature waiting for wolves, I see huge herds of bison passing in front of me, foxes chasing mice, prairie dogs peering cheekily from their burrows and uttering a shrill warning whistle at the sight of me. I watch moose calves stalking after their mothers on their thin legs, I see martens darting up trees, and am amazed by the size of a beaver dragging branches to its lodge. There are such an incredible amount of species in Yellowstone, not to mention the other natural phenomena like the hot springs and geysers and the view of the Milky Way at night. None of this makes me forget the wolves, but it makes me grateful that the wolves sometimes keep me waiting for so long that I have time to discover nature. The wolves have given me an eye for detail, and thus also an eye for seeing other animals and plants. Seeing them, and observing how everything fits together and lives together, without any influence from humans, makes me feel humble and happy.

We humans are insignificant to this planet. But we are part of this earth and should therefore behave as if it is the most important thing for us. If we go on living as we are, we will not only destroy our climate and our natural resources, we will destroy ourselves. Nature won't care if man disappears. It will just make room for the next invention. It will open a new page in the book of life. As a vital part of a fully functional ecosystem, the wolf can remind us that our two species not only share the same habitat, but also the same fate.

Wolf Medicine

How the Magic of Wolves Can Heal Us

Early one spring morning, when the road from Mammoth Hot Springs to the Old Faithful geyser was cleared for traffic for the first time that year, I drove to the Norris Geyser Basin. I love the time when I'm alone and can pursue my own thoughts. Norris is one of my favourite places. Here I feel close to the belly of Mother Earth. In this area the earth's crust is only 5 kilometres thick (normally it's about 50). Yellowstone is a slumbering super-volcano. The land has a particular power because the unbounded possibilities of nature are alive there. Norris is the hottest place in the park, and is formed of fire and ice. Sometimes things happen very slowly here – in terms of geological timescales – and sometimes they happen in a flash. It's a place where creation is never-ending.

I was sitting on a tree trunk in the middle of gurgling, seething, hissing hot springs. Rivers and streams exhaled clouds of steam among cold fields of snow, warm streams that looked out of place in an Arctic environment. The sun struggled to find a way to the water coloured red and blue by minerals. In the distance I heard squeaking, whimpering and screeching sounds.

They rose and transformed into a high-pitched laugh, the trill of an operatic diva. Coyotes! My wild friends. They were singing their morning song, their prayer to the sun.

A reply from behind me followed promptly. Deeper. Calmer. Longer. From powerful throats. I turned round in slow motion. A light-grey wolf stood only about 5 metres away, looking at me. By his bristling hackles I could tell he was a young animal. His ears pricked forward curiously. His tail, slightly raised, showed uncertainty. My camera was on the ground next to me, but I refrained from reaching for it. That would have broken the spell. I held my breath. My heartbeat roared in my ears. We looked at each other.

Yellow eyes plunged into blue eyes. Seconds. Minutes. Then a bird flew up beside me and startled me. The wolf took a step back, turned round and ran off. I sat there for a long time trying to understand that moment. A moment of eternity.

A few hours later I was standing by the road in Lamar Valley observing the Druid pack when a yellow school bus full of young people pulled into the lay-by. The looks we wolf-watchers gave each other spoke volumes. In my experience, so many young people would mean there was a general lack of interest among them, noise and anarchy. With their unbridled energy they would chase the wolves away. But we were mistaken. When the driver opened the door, teachers and children got out silently and in a disciplined fashion, and joined us. We quietly gave them a quick overview about the wolf family we were watching.

'There are really wolves there?' asked two gangly girls with nose piercings who were starting to shiver in the cold under their thin jackets.

'Yes. do you want to look?' I set my scope on the wolves and let all the students look through it. One after another they came forward and watched the playing Druids through the lens.

'Wow!'

'Cool!'

'They are soooo beautiful,' sighed one of the girls with tears in her eyes.

'Real wolves!'

The teenagers were fascinated. Then the wolves started howling. The young people froze and listened open-mouthed.

'These are their first wolves,' the teacher said with a smile, and thanked me for helping with the scopes.

When they all drove off and waved goodbye I was ashamed of my prejudices, and practised humility again.

Two wolf encounters that couldn't be more different. And yet they both had the same magic. An encounter with a wild wolf leaves no one cold. It touches something deep within us, a place where we are still whole.

Indigenous peoples know that too. I spent almost a year living in the wilderness in Minnesota in a cabin without electricity or running water, right in the middle of wolf and bear territory. The property abutted the land of the Ojibwa Indians. One day when I was hiking through the woods I met Henry Smallwood 'Big Wolf', an Ojibwa medicine man. The powerful grey-haired man had a Clark Gable moustache, and the thin strip of hair, like his old-fashioned steel-rimmed glasses, looked lost in his round face. Henry told me that for his tribe there was no difference between them and the wolves. 'The wolf keeps knowledge and teaches humility. The great creator first created a circle, and everything else found room in it afterwards. That's why everything moves in a circle: man, from childhood to death, the seasons, the stars, sun, moon, Earth – everything is round.' The medicine man, whose polo shirt stretched over his belly, and who couldn't close the zip of his windbreaker jacket, laughed. 'Take a look at me. I'm round too.'

He went on: 'There's a universal rhythm. Wolves are the brothers of men. We men couldn't survive without animals. We owe them something. At ceremonies in honour of wolves we give it back to them by singing for them.'

For many indigenous peoples wolves are of great significance. They identify with them as kindred souls, dress up in wolf hides at ceremonies and respect the predators.

For the Ojibwa the wolf is medicine. He brings them back to balance.

It's easy to see that we all long for this harmony as well: city-dwellers wear T-shirts with a picture of a wild animal or outdoor clothing with the logo of a wolf's paw print, while driving to the office in petrol-guzzling, CO_2-spewing four-by-fours. We like things that represent the wilderness to us, and think that if we wear or drive them we'll manage to get them back. We've become alienated from nature and the wilds. In our high-tech age, we don't even experience darkness and silence any more. Is it possible that we're deliberately grieving for something that we think is lost?

For many people wolves, bears and lynx are a symbol of the wilderness. They think a landscape without wolves is missing something and they long to see them. In our digital era wolves are something real. They represent life and death, real nature without fences between us.

There are no longer very many places where you can experience something like that. Yellowstone is one such place. Nine thousand square kilometres of untouched nature, interrupted only by a single road that snakes in a figure of eight around the sights and the hotels. Those who don't find that lonely enough just need to park their cars and walk along one of the many hiking paths into the backcountry. But don't forget your bear spray: this is the *real* wilderness!

Since prehistoric times humans have gone into nature to reflect on things, to find answers or get to know themselves. I too need my regular downtime. I go hiking in Arizona through the Grand Canyon, I paddle in the Boundary Waters of Minnesota, admire the Northern Lights of Alaska or observe the wolves in Yellowstone. In nature I experience four and a half billion years of success – the best of everything, the most sublime that the earth has to offer. Go into nature and you are surrounded by victors.

But we are all the more vulnerable precisely because the wilderness can be threatening. In my cabin in Minnesota I lived 30 kilometres from the nearest town, and had to walk 8 kilometres along a narrow path to reach my car on the road. There was neither a phone network nor a radio connection. One stroke of the axe into my leg when chopping wood and I could have bled to death. That's a risk you have to take when you opt for loneliness. To coin a phrase: wilderness isn't for cowards. It can be a cruel master that trips up the reckless and the inexperienced. People who have grown up in and with nature are rarely looking for adventure. If they expose themselves to risky situations of their own free will, it often happens for spiritual reasons, as was the case with Robert Stanley, whom I met in the Hayden Valley.

There are two kinds of tourists who visit Yellowstone. Some want to see the geysers and the hot springs, and 'catch' a grizzly or a wolf in passing so that they can talk about it at home. And there are those who are in search of something. I see it in their eyes when they observe a wolf. One such person was Robert. We stood side by side for a long time in a lay-by watching the Canyon wolf family with their white female leader. Robert didn't seem to notice the other tourists, he was concentrating so hard on the wolves. It was only when they had moved on, and the two-legged visitors with them, that we fell into conversation. He told me his remarkable life story, and how the wolves had saved him.

In June 1969 Robert had been deployed in north Vietnam as a sergeant with the Green Berets, a US army special unit. He spent eighteen months in uninterrupted fighting.

'I felt as if I had seen and experienced the true definition of the word "hell",' he told me.

After a serious injury from a shell he was granted extended sick leave. 'I wanted to get as far as possible from people, into total isolation,' he said. He took the bare minimum that he needed to survive and flew to Fairbanks, Alaska. He drove his rental car east and set up camp in the wilderness. For the first few weeks he hardly saw anything but a few animals and a lot of tracks. He heard wolves howling, but couldn't find any.

'I wasn't afraid. I'd experienced the most horrible cruelties that people can do to one another. At that point I almost wished I was dead. I could no longer live with the horror I'd been cursed to see. One crystal-clear night, I looked up to the sky in a desperate cry for a higher being, whether it be God, Allah, Rama, Buddha or whoever. I pleaded for an answer to questions to which I was sure there were no answers. Late that night I heard the long call of a wolf. It sounded like a soul calling to me. The only time I had ever heard such a lonely call was that of my own soul. I thought: *whoever you are, we have so much to cry about.*' Exhausted, he fell asleep.

The next morning Robert saw a white wolf watching him from some distance away. He didn't feel threatened. In the course of the next few days the wolf always appeared in the same spot. Over time it came close enough for Robert to see that it was a female. He started talking to her. Then, one night, she approached him and sat down only a few metres away from him. A few days later the wolf stood in front of him with her tail between her legs and her head lowered.

'I stretched out my hand and touched my white goddess. She became my guardian angel. I needed her so much. She took my

The white female leader of the Canyon pack

life back to a state that I could deal with. She saved my life and stopped me going mad.'

There was a man standing next to me who had experienced the most terrible horror of war, and it was an Arctic wolf that had given him new hope and a new life when he needed it most. Robert's story shows how wolves can heal even a trauma-tized soul.

In Frazier Park, California, about an hour and a half's drive from Los Angeles, is the Lockwood Animal Rescue Center (LARC). Here, on a piece of land with an area of about 12 square kilometres, live injured and abused wolves and wolf hybrids saved by Matthew Simmons, a former marine. He offers a pro-gramme for war veterans suffering from post-traumatic stress disorder (PTSD).

In LARC soldiers can work with wolves, feed them, clean their enclosures and develop a relationship with them. The suf-fering of returning war veterans is often deliberately ignored by American society, and they receive little support. The vets go to the psychologist, to special PTSD seminars or take drugs to escape their experiences. Twenty-two of them commit suicide every day. A programme like this one is often their last chance. There's a long waiting list.

'The soldiers and the wolves have the same fate,' says Matthew Simmons. 'They have both been abused in the past. Now they have to learn to trust again.'

'If you're somewhere where people want to kill you, it changes you,' a veteran says in the documentary about LARC, *The War in Between*.

It can take traumatized men and women a long time to establish a bond with the wolves, sometimes months. And then it's usually just a single wolf that seeks out 'their' human – a lesson in patience and acceptance.

'Just because I haven't got something under control, it doesn't need to drive me mad,' says one former soldier. 'I can feed the wolves and clean the enclosures, but I can't make them do something they don't want to do. They're not dogs.'

Abused wolves and war veterans trust one another; they build up a relationship and heal one another.

Another tale of a miraculous healing by wild wolves is told by the biologist Gudrun Pflüger in her book *Wolf Spirit*.*

For the indigenous inhabitants of Canada, the First Nation, the wolf is a creature that establishes a connection between time and space. The wolf appears only when he has something to communicate to us. Gudrun Pflüger had a close encounter with wolves in Canada, which produced fantastic footage showing them sniffing at her as she lies in the grass. But the biologist, who was already suffering from an undiagnosed and aggressive brain

---

* *Wolfspirit: Meine Geschichte von Wölfen und Wundern*, Munich, 2014

tumour, which she only found out about after her journey, is convinced that the wolves wanted to give her some of their strength and resilience on her odyssey through the illness. Even in the worst times of her cancer treatment Gudrun Pflüger never thought of giving up. She wanted to see her four-legged friends again.

Biologically, we could explain the sniffing by saying that the wolves smelled a chemical imbalance in her body. (You remember the bison cow in Wolf Park that developed pneumonia a week after its meeting with the wolves?) But that's insignificant. The important thing is that a bond arose between Gudrun Pflüger and the animals which healed her soul.

I've also experienced such a sense of healing several times. Whenever death or tragedies have entered my life, I have found comfort in the wilderness of Yellowstone. In a place where I can touch 50-million-year-old petrified trees and where, beneath my feet, a huge chamber of glowing magma seethes, I feel tiny. Not insignificant – on the contrary. Here I can see myself as part of the whole, as part of the big plan of things. That gives me a deep feeling of peace.

Why do we seek comfort in nature? Why do we feel so good when we see, hear, smell or feel animals? When we consider a tree and smell the scent of flowers? When we look at a rushing river or a calm sea?

I am never alone outside in nature, and I never feel lonely. When I sit on my favourite hill and look out over Lamar Valley, I sometimes catch my breath at the sight of so much magnificence, wonder and variety. There is a timelessness in extreme beauty. The present doesn't disappear; it becomes eternity.

We need such experiences of the wilderness to learn to be at home in our lives, to feel what it's like to be alive.

When I guide people to the wolves in Yellowstone, I am aware of something mysterious happening to them when they hear the howling of a wolf or look into its eyes. Something familiar. They see something that is in all of us, something that we know but have perhaps already lost. Something we fear, but to which we feel drawn.

Such moments change us. With wolves (and other wild animals) we experience an intense moment. We are ourselves, not who we were or want to be, or how we represent ourselves through the amount of money in our bank account or on our social media profile. An animal doesn't see in us the image that we wish to present to the outside world, but what we actually are: aggression, anxiety, insecurity, happiness or serenity. Wolves have the ability to notice our hidden emotions; we are transparent to them – and thus at their mercy.

Not everyone can withdraw into the wilderness to meet wolves. But all of us, if we are open, can experience the wisdom of wolves within ourselves and meet the wolf inside us. I was able to experience this in a shamanic seminar.

At the risk of you wanting to put me in the esoteric corner after the following description, I would like to tell you about an experience that turned my world on its head.

In the autumn of 2008 I received an invitation to go to a weekend shamanic seminar in Bavaria, in which participants were to learn to use the power and knowledge of wolves in their lives. The seminar was organized by Willee Regensburger, who lives near Lake Chiemsee in Bavaria and who was initiated as a shaman in Korea. His current teacher is a spiritual leader of the Lakota Indians in Pine Ridge Reservation, South Dakota.

My task was to provide information about wolves and explain and interpret the experiences of the participants, so I was almost a wolfish interpreter. I confess that I was more than sceptical. Admittedly I wasn't a newcomer to mystical matters, particularly since in the 1980s I had spent three winters living in Santa Fe, New Mexico, the spiritual capital of the USA at the time.

But this was something quite new to me. I was to compare the experiences of men and women acquired in the shamanic process with my knowledge and experience of wolves.

For three days, under Willee's leadership, the participants undertook various spiritual soul-journeys to their spirit animals. They drummed, danced, howled and made wolf masks out of plaster.

One of the exercises dealt with the hunting strategies of wolves. Through shamanic drumming, everyone was led into a deep meditative state and sent on a spiritual journey. There they were to move and hunt like a wolf. What they reported of their experiences still gives me goosebumps. Elisabeth, a Bavarian farmer and herbalist, who had never seen a wolf in her life except in a zoo, gave a detailed description of how she – as a wolf – had hunted and taken down an elk cow. She described her hunt as a hungry wolf:

'I ran off; I didn't care what was happening around me. The animal kicked me. I felt no pain. Nothing existed now apart from my hunger and the animal I wanted to kill. I sank my teeth into its throat and tasted the blood. When the animal fell and was lying in the grass, I tore large pieces of flesh out of it. It tasted so good. At last I could eat my fill. It felt warm and good.'

The descriptions of the other participants were also startlingly similar to the real lives of wolves. These were events that you can't observe among captive wolves in zoos. These wolves can't kill living prey. You only see something like that among wild wolves. Only a few experts know the details, and they were being described by laypeople. I was surprised and fascinated.

The big wolf dance in the evening was the highlight of the event. The participants put on the wolf masks they had made and, to the sound of the drums, transformed into a pack of wolves. I know the songs of wolves. This sounded spookily authentic. These were no longer human voices imitating wolves, these humans *were* wolves, and I felt as if I were standing in the middle of a pack. The poor farmers on the nearby farms probably had some very startled cattle in their byres that night.

Whatever your views on the subject of shamanism, it is definitely an experience that has a great deal to teach those who are willing to open themselves up to it. The seminar convinced me that we already have all the knowledge about wolves, animals, nature and the wilderness within us, and can bring it out at any time. The participants didn't just get to know predators, they experienced themselves as wolves and thus acquired a better understanding of these animals and their lives. Meetings with wild wolves – whether real or spiritual – change us to the very core of our being.

Wolves and the wilderness lead us to ask the existential spiritual questions. Who am I? Why am I here? What's the meaning of life? We sense in us a spark of the divine that all animals carry within themselves. Except wolves don't ask themselves those questions. They aren't interested in whether they are our spirit animals or not, or if we want to build an altar to them, or whether we hate them. They aren't even interested in whether we exist or not. We're just a part of their environment, to which they adapt.

Perhaps that is their greatest gift to us: that insignificance, the unimportance of humans to wolves. Perhaps we need to show greater humility and modesty in our response to nature. It's time for us to stop taking ourselves so seriously and just *be*. Then we'll be closer to wolves than we have ever been.

Of Men and Wolves

A Difficult Relationship Between Love and Hate

Imagine the following scene: a small group of wolves sits round a conference table holding a discussion. They come from all over the world. They are intelligent and cultured and particularly well versed in the biology of the notorious biped species *Homo sapiens*. They are here to talk about their relationship with human beings over the past few thousand years. What do you think they will say?

Perhaps they will get worked up about the horrific deeds of the human race and the war crimes carried out against their lupine forefathers. They could also make fun of the bizarre ideas that humans have, and the bipeds' confusion about fact and fiction in their relationship with them, the wolves. Perhaps one or other of the participants might express admiration for the way in which early humans respected wolves, imitated their lives in family groups and in hunting together. And the quickly growing popularity of wolves among bipeds would certainly be another point of discussion. After an exhausting overview of wolf–human relations they all reach the conclusion that there are so many individuals and different facets involved that it's impossible to generalize.

We humans reach the same conclusion when we engage intensely with wolves over a long period of time. There are so many different aspects of the wolf–human relationship that it isn't possible to speak in general terms, just as we can't speak about *the* wolf as such. In the end the wolf exists in the eye of the beholder. There is the wolf as described by science, but there is also the wolf who exists in human minds: a construction created from our individual, cultural or social conditioning. This wolf is the sum of everything we know about the animal and how we want it to be. And what comes into play here is precisely what has made our lives difficult from the start, and not only when dealing with wolves: our prejudices.

We all have certain resentments – be they towards foreigners, Muslims, homosexuals, working women, the heirs of wealthy families . . . The list could go on for ever. Let's add the wolf to it. Prejudices are a deeply human quality, and are firmly anchored in the brain. At the same time they have nothing to do with reality. They are basically a trick of the mind in order to save energy in the processing of information. The quicker a human being can arrange their surroundings, the more capacity remains for other thought processes, and the quicker they can react to dangers. However, if prejudices are internalized, it is difficult to get rid of them again because they assume control over the processing of information – and thus repeatedly confirm themselves. The fact is that we need 'pre-judgements' for our orientation through life. If we analysed all the things we experience individually, it would put too much of a strain on us. For that reason, in our perception we rely on simplifying matters and arranging them into categories.

Prejudices are complex and diverse and hence difficult to shake off. Consequently man's attitude to wolves is generally influenced from childhood onwards. Many myths and stories, including the one about the little girl with the red hood who is eaten by him, have shaped our image of the 'big bad wolf'. And, not least, the opinion of the population is easily influenced by false or inadequate reports in the media. Negative attitudes make it hard to find a compromise between human interests and the protection of species.

In my talks and lectures I find time and again that the symbolic status of the wolf as the 'bad wolf' is still so firmly rooted in people's minds that biological facts are often irrelevant. Real numbers, for example whether and how many people have been killed by wolves, are not correctly perceived. In Europe over the last fifty years nine people have been killed by wolves: five by animals suffering from rabies and four children in Spain who were playing near a village where wolves had been fed. However, some people remain convinced that the wolf is lurking behind the nearest hedge waiting to eat an innocent child.

The risk of being injured or killed by a wolf is minimal. If you are afraid of a wolf, you should leave your car in the drive, because you are much more likely to be killed in a car accident than by a wolf. I also advise you not to fly, or be outside in a storm, because there is a higher possibility that you will be killed. You certainly shouldn't cross a field of cows, because more people are killed by cows every year than by great white sharks. But the most dangerous thing of all is probably your office job; in Germany alone 300 people a year choke on ballpoint pens! The wolf does not feature among the twenty animals responsible for the greatest number of human deaths, while dogs are at number four and man in first place. You see, there are greater dangers than wolves.

Thanks to constant educational efforts in the present day, luckily there are more and more people who claim not to be afraid of wolves. But if you ask them directly whether they would mind if a pack of wolves lived in their local city forest, the answer comes back like a pistol shot: 'No! That's not what I meant at all.

In the city forest? Then we couldn't go walking there with the children!' Wolves, yes, but not outside our front door, would seem to be the feeling.

Fear is the illness of our time, the one we struggle with the most. Fear of the enemy, the outsider, the neighbour, the self, power, love and other things. Perhaps the wolf then is only another symbol for everything that is frightening and evil.

Fear of the wolf was another of the main reasons for the destruction of whole wolf populations. Every educated person today knows that wolves don't eat people. And yet we look anxiously over our shoulders when we go walking in a forest where wolves live. Wasn't that a twig snapping? (For your information: wolves move silently; nothing snaps.) Was that a shadow? The human fear of wolves is etched deeply in our genes. 'It is biologically programmed, like the fear of spiders and snakes,' says the evolutionary psychologist Harald A. Euler. To be afraid of them it's enough to see someone else being frightened. Many people who suffer from wolf phobias have had no negative experiences themselves, or the chance to experience whether these animals are really as dangerous as they seem. And yet they are quick to form an opinion.

The absurd – and worrying – traits that prejudices can assume are apparent in the experience of Manuela L.*, one of my seminar participants.

It was still the early morning when Manuela took her dogs for a walk from her holiday home in a little town in Saxony-Anhalt. For the first time in many years she had planned a holiday in Germany. She had sought the town out on a map of German wolf territories. It was supposed to be in the middle of a wolf territory. Manuela hoped to meet a wild wolf for the first

* Name changed.

time in her life, or at least to hear one howling. 'Just feeling that they could be nearby was so exciting,' she said to me with gleaming eyes. So that morning she packed her binoculars in her rucksack, put her dogs on the leash and set off. While her thirteen-year-old Boston terrier mix Emma stayed near her mistress, her four-year-old Hovawart mix Freya stretched the 10-metre retractable leash to its full length and snuffled eagerly about the bushes.

Suddenly Manuela heard a frightened woman's voice. 'Th-there's a wolf coming!'

And a male voice answered: 'No, no, it's just a dog.'

A little later an elderly couple appeared on the hiking path. They were both wearing hiking trousers and jackets, and carried backpacks. Freya had hurried back to her mistress long ago.

The woman apologized. 'I'm sorry. I thought your dog was a wolf.'

'Do you really think it's possible to see a real wolf here?' Manuela asked, her heart thumping. Perhaps she was about to get some more concrete information. Instead the couple exploded with fury.

'Those vile creatures. A forester I know had this hunting dog that was laying under the perch, and they actually tore him to pieces.' The man's face turned purple and the veins in his forehead stood out as he continued. 'Not far from here they ripped a whole herd of over a hundred mouflon apart and left them lying there dead.' His voice broke as he roared at Manuela, who took a step back. 'When will something finally be done around here? The politicians need to intervene. But the damned animal-rights lunatics and the tree-huggers have far too strong a lobby.'

His wife nodded in agreement, her glasses almost falling off her nose.

'Nobody can walk with children in the forest these days,' she raged. 'Over in the farms the farmers' wives can't leave their babies unattended in the buggy in the yard. As soon as the little thing starts crying, the wolves get all excited and come and drag it out of the buggy.' Her eyes filled with tears – whether out of pity for the child or fury about the bloodthirsty creatures who lie in wait for innocent children, Manuela couldn't tell.

'It'll have to come to that before something is done here,' the woman went on, now glaring furiously at Emma and Freya, who were now lying down beside Manuela – almost 'deputizing' for the murderous predators. 'An expert told me that, a hunter,' the woman said stoutly.

Manuela suddenly felt as if she had been catapulted back to the Middle Ages and decided to respond to the hikers' remarks only with a non-committal nod. She took the dog leads and was about to continue on her way.

But the man, who seemed to be of the opinion that he had to outdo his wife in terms of drama, reached behind him to his belt and pulled out a pistol.

'We haven't gone for a walk in the forest for months without this,' he shouted, waving the gun around in front of Manuela, who moved her animals behind her as inconspicuously as possible.

The man went on ranting. 'If I encounter one of those beasts, I will make quick work of it and bury the body in the forest. Then I won't even give a damn about those crazy conservationists with their tracking devices. My friend the hunter always says that's the only reason why the hunting fraternity isn't taking tough action right now.'

Manuela feigned ignorance. 'What? I don't understand.'

'Well, the conservationists can keep track of every step the wolves take. If you're caught shooting them, it can get expensive.'

'Karl! Put that thing away,' his wife said, pushing down the hand holding the gun. 'You're frightening the young woman.'

He did so. And later, when Manuela had walked a little way away from the pair, she wondered what would have happened if the man had shared his wife's view that Freya was a wolf. If he had, the dog would be dead.

Manuela was still worked up when she described her experience. I asked her if she was going to take another 'wolf holiday'.

'I don't think so!' she replied. 'We're going to safer places from now on. And I don't mean safe from wolves; I mean safe from humans.'

I assume that while reading this description you'll have been shaking your head with disbelief. But they still exist – prejudices, ignorance and intolerance. They are the main threats to the existence of wolves.

The primal demons of our childhood leave no one indifferent. Because their domesticated siblings have been sharing our households for thousands of years, wolves are more familiar to us than any other animal. We love them or hate them. They are strangers, and as such they are already a threat. 'They don't belong in our world, and they were exterminated for good reason. Wolves belong in the wilderness, man in the cultivated landscape. The two can't live together.' And that at least is what people say these days. And also: 'We have nothing against wolves, but only where they don't bother anybody.' This is followed by the most ludicrous suggestions, such as taking wolves into the Bavarian Forest or other nature reserves and 'somehow' ensuring they stay there. Maybe fencing them in? Apart from the fact that is impossible for purely practical reasons, this would mean a zoo and not a wilderness. Keeping bears, wolves and lynx as 'symbols of the wilderness' behind bars, with human beings in control of everything – is that how we imagine nature?

The wolves are quite a way ahead of us in that respect, because they do not distinguish between wilderness and cultivated landscape, which seems so important to us. Wolves live in our midst, adapting to our world. As long as there is enough prey and a place to hide, the synanthropic ('living near humans' or 'cultural follower') wolf can live anywhere – and it usually does that entirely unnoticed.

But we humans have different opinions about what wilderness really means, and the wolves seem to be caught in the middle. The opponents of wolves want to send them back into nature, away from humans, while the friends of wolves hold the view that wolves *and* humans are both part of nature.

'Nature' and 'wilderness' mean as many different things as 'man' or 'wolf'. But what 'wilderness' absolutely doesn't mean is being free of human design. For several thousand years there has been no nature without the influence and presence of human beings. The wilderness adapted to us long ago. Because of the clear-cutting of the forests and the huge rise in areas under cultivation, wild animals are driven out of their natural habitat and forced into the cities. In Berlin today there is a greater variety of breeding birds than in the Eifel National Park. Raccoons, wild boar and foxes can become a 'problem' in the city. They learn quickly that a fast-food-filled rubbish bin is easier to empty than a rabbit is to catch, and that you can sleep comfortably in a garden shed. So animals do what they have always done – they adapt – and they still don't quite fit.

The biggest wolf populations in Germany live on active military training areas or abandoned surface mines, all of which owe their existence to human influence and are as biodiverse and 'wild' as almost any terrain. Even in Chernobyl, twenty-five years after the nuclear accident, an astonishing diversity of plants and animals now get on with their lives – including a large and healthy wolf population. They have all adapted to the extreme radiation and enjoy the peace and remoteness. But that isn't what we imagine when we think of nature and wilderness either.

We try in vain to tame nature and keep it in check. But we never leave it in peace. Our society has assumed a kind of control over nature that would have been unthinkable only a century ago. People don't want wilderness, they want safety. They go for walks in the wolf territory as if they were going into war: pepper spray in their belts, whistles in their jacket pockets and iPhones at the ready for a possible emergency call – and heaven help them if the signal fails.

A lot of people feel a deep emotional connection with wolves, seeing them as beautiful, intelligent and highly social animals who must be defended against the attacks of those who disagree. According to this, the wolf, holy, pure, honest and authentic, is a victim of a civilization who wants to subjugate nature.

Such ideas of the wolf do not accord with reality. As predators wolves hunt and kill their prey, and that also includes livestock if it is not guarded. And, yes, there have been attacks on humans, even if they have been extremely rare and unusual. Often wolf-romantics refuse to admit this. Instead it is sometimes represented as if the fact that wolves hunt or kill other animals is mere coincidence.

The image of wolves as hunters that don't simply kill with a 'clean' bite to the throat, but start devouring their prey while it is still alive, don't match the rosy image of the wolf as sacred spiritual kin.

The love of nature that a lot of people feel when confronted with wolves is based on an idealized vision of nature that is problematic. Both haters and romantics see the animal from their personal perspective, through their own ideas and ideologies, instead of perceiving it realistically. It's easy to have deep feelings for a majestic animal like a wolf, but difficult to reconcile those feelings with the knowledge that wolves have a function as top-level predators, that creatures are eaten by other creatures, and that man is, in the end, a predator too.

What we lack is a realistic, objective view of the wolf. Because, in fact, it's only a perfectly ordinary animal. If we want to live with wolves, we have to approach the situation rationally and realistically and separate facts from fiction. Only then can wolves and humans coexist.

But how do we do that? I asked the photographer and wildlife cameraman Jim Brandenburg. When I moved to the wilderness of Minnesota in 1992, Jim was a distant neighbour. In the town of Ely there was a gallery showing his photographs, where we fell into conversation about wolves and prejudices. I had previously founded the Society for the Protection of Wolves with Günther Bloch to educate people about the wolves who would only officially arrive in Germany eight years later. But since individually emigrating wolves who kept coming were being shot illegally, we wanted to do something. Jim gave me a valuable piece of advice: 'If you want to persuade people of something, you have to come in through the back door. You can't just march in through the front door. That applies to everything in our lives – giving up smoking, drinking, driving too fast, killing wolves. People are willing to change, but you have to use the back door.'

Basically my work is a search for the back door in people's heads and hearts. We only protect what we love, and only love what we know. So apart from sound factual knowledge we also need an emotional connection with wolves. One of the most beautiful ways to get there leads through direct encounters with them.

The Italian ecologist and wolf researcher Luigi Boitani recommended aptly in an interview: 'Take people to places where wolves live. Let them listen to the animals howling at night. Show them the carcasses of wolf kills, tracks, scats – show them everything.'

That's my experience too. In order to see wolves realistically, we have to go into their world. It isn't enough to fit them with a GPS collar and follow their movements on a computer monitor. And it isn't enough to watch a wildlife video. And we'll gain even less of an understanding of the wolf if we watch them through the fence of an enclosure. To understand wolves as a whole, as the autonomous personalities they are, we must go to them. By that I don't mean that we should force ourselves on them, but that we should approach as detached, patient observers. We need to get dirty and cold, practise the high art of patience and leave them alone.

Really getting to know and understand wolves doesn't mean that we should sit and relax in the sun all day, camera and notebook on our knees, and smile as we watch playing pups. It means watching sleeping wolves for several hours at minus 30 degrees and waiting longingly for an ear or the tip of a tail to twitch. And, yes, then we smile (and shiver with cold) as we watch the waking wolf family.

Observing wolves also means enduring harshness, cruelty, killed prey animals, blood and broken bones. Watching wolves taking down an elk – or another wolf you have learned to love – can be so brutal that you want to close your eyes or run away. But then that is life. Anyone who just wants to see playing pups or the wolves who look after them, who seeks the 'sacred', the bright and beautiful, is wasting their time in the wilderness. They would be better off going to a zoo or watching a National Geographic film from which the ugliest scenes have been cut.

I once visited the whale festival in Sitka, Alaska. Along with the biologists I went out to sea on a boat and watched with fascinated horror as a group of orcas hunted the calf of a grey whale, separated it from its desperate mother and killed it. In their family structure and pack hunting strategies orcas and wolves are very similar. It's no coincidence that killer whales are also called 'sea wolves'.

If we want to understand the fascination of wolves, we mustn't close our eyes to the darkness. Only when we accept nature with all its facets will we learn that we have long carried it in our hearts.

Welcome Wolf

Living with Wolves in Germany

Late January 2017: I was in search of wolves again – not in far-away Wyoming this time, but in Germany. Along with four friends, I had gone tracking in Lower Saxony. We had all been together in Yellowstone several times, and had watched wolves there. It was clear to us that our chances of seeing one of the predators here were vanishingly small, but it was enough for us to know they were there, because we were in the middle of the territory of a wolf family. We had undertaken our trip on a question we hoped we would be able to answer in the end: Why do we need wolves?

The four-house hamlet of Dübekold is about 30 kilometres in a straight line from Gorleben on the edge of Göhrde State Forest in the district of Lüchow-Dannenberg in Lower Saxony. The Göhrde is the largest uninterrupted mixed forest area in north Germany, and home to several wolves who occasionally, and involuntarily, startle walkers (or fascinate them, depending on who you talk to). We were in this forest that morning. It had recently snowed, and the hope of a track or at least some howling was high. Our wolf adviser and guide was Kenny Kenner, who works as a wolf ambassador with NABU (Nature and Bio-diversity Conservation Union) in matters of herd protection for livestock breeders. He had found a fresh deer carcass the previous day, and wolf tracks nearby.

We set off on our quest. For four hours we marched through the forest and across fields, mostly keeping our eyes on the ground and looking over our shoulders every now and again so that we didn't miss a wolf that might secretly have appeared behind us. But presumably we were making too much noise for that. Five people plus a guide with a dog won't be able to hide themselves from a wolf. But we were still contented. On a forest path we found a line of tracks: a trail with a sequence of prints, a stride length of 1.22 metres, each paw print 8 centimetres long (without claws) and 7 centimetres wide. We also discovered traces of urine and – hurray! – several little scats containing hair and bones. Kenny grabbed his out of his bag, took samples of scats with a spatula and put them in a small jar of alcohol to send them for DNA examination, noted and photographed the site of the find and the surrounding area, and in passing explained to us the fauna and flora as well as the history of wolves in the Göhrde.

They had been here: a pair of parents and six young wolves. Perhaps they were even watching us from the bushes. All our mental antennae were switched to receive. The awareness of being in wolf territory made us much more awake and alive than usual.

A few years ago I could never have imagined going in search of wolves in Germany. To see the big predators I had to fly to the USA. Now at last I could also find them in my homeland. Things had come full circle.

But not everyone is as happy about the presence of wolves as I am. Even today the wolf is a creature of conflict and arouses passionate reactions, from scepticism to sheer terror. As I wrote in the last chapter, shepherds are worried about their animals, hunters about their deer and joggers about their safety. There are still wolf wars. While wars were previously waged *against* wolves, nowadays they are being waged *about* wolves in a variety of campaigns on different eco-political fronts.

In areas where the basic food resource of the population is dependent on livestock, people are afraid. Sheep, cattle and horse breeders don't know how to protect their animals, or how to apply for grants or compensation. The return of wolves has made their lives more complicated. For them, the predator represents a world in which city-dwellers and animal-lovers ride roughshod over the rights and needs of the rural population and try to force their own idea of nature on them. That does not exactly make them friends of wolves and their advocates, because wolves can be very difficult neighbours.

The first sign that they live near us is usually dead sheep. Wolves are opportunists and eat what they can easily kill. That includes unprotected livestock like sheep or calves, not because wolves want to 'annoy' us or destroy our livelihoods, but because we've offered them to them as food. Once they have learned that unguarded sheep are easy prey, they will repeatedly choose them for food. And to be quite honest I can't blame them. Would you go into the forest and hunt your own steak if it was being handed to you on a plate? It would insult the intelligence of wolves to assume that they would turn down such a thing.

A livestock keeper must learn to think like a wolf and protect his animals accordingly. This is best done with a combination of wolf-proof electric fence and livestock-guarding dogs. These big, strong breeds have been used for thousands of years in southern and eastern European countries with wolves to protect sheep and cattle. They defend them as their 'pack'. Other herd-protection species are donkeys and llamas.

Yes, that kind of protection is elaborate and expensive. But it is sponsored and promoted by the German government, and a livestock breeder will be compensated for animals killed by a wolf, as long as the requisite protective measures have been taken for his animals. That is the real price of living in a wolf territory. The wolf doesn't come free.

If wolves force their way into a herd of sheep and kill several animals, the shock and rage of the owners is entirely understandable. Yet the perpetrator is not a 'bloodthirsty mass murderer'. In terms of the ecology of behaviour, that doesn't make sense either – why should predators destroy their own basic food resources?

In the rare phenomenon of what is known as surplus killing, it can be seen that wolves, like the notorious 'fox in the henhouse', will go on attacking until nothing is moving. How many prey animals a wolf kills at once and how much of their prey they eats depends among other things on how easy the sheep are to catch and whether the wolf is disturbed by humans. Grazing animals are sometimes crammed too tightly behind a fence, can't escape and are therefore easy prey for a wolf.

Normally wolves eat as much of a carcass as they can. In this particular case, however, the wolf doesn't get to eat because they are being repeatedly interrupted by all the sheep running around, and their hunting reflex is unleashed again each time. The slaughtered animals lie where they are. Surplus killings are very rare among wild animals.

At a nature conference I fell into conversation with shepherds who complained that they would soon have to give up rearing their animals because they 'were only feeding wolves'. They couldn't afford protective measures, they said. 'While I'm busy filling in forms the wolf will calmly get on with eating my sheep. We don't need wolves, any more than we need martens, cormorants or ravens,' a young shepherd growled at me. 'The wolf had died out and that was fine.'

★

Humans, who see themselves as the crown of creation, and as the only ones allowed to decide which animals have a right to life, are not in a position (or willing) to recognize ecological contexts. They resist any kind of change and thus block themselves. If they opened up and adapted to the new situation, they might often receive remarkable help – for example from the wolves themselves.

One fascinating and little-known phenomenon is the fact that even wolves can be a good 'protection' for sheep. Wolves generally eat what their parents and grandparents have taught them is 'safe' food ('food imprinting'). In Germany that is red deer, roe deer and wild boar. In Saxony wild ungulates constitute 94.9 per cent of the food eaten by wolves. If they have never had positive experiences with the meat of sheep or calves, wolves aren't interested in those prey species. One shepherd I talked to at the conference uses that knowledge to his advantage. He makes the wolves 'work' for him. He told me proudly about 'his' wolf pack.

'The seven wolves live very close by. Every now and again I see them walking past the sheep and marking their territory.' One of the wolves had once tested the electric fence and established that sheep 'bite'. He had plainly made that clear to his family as well, because the shepherd didn't lose a single one of his sheep to the wolves. However, they defended their territory against fellow wolves from outside their territory. 'It was the best thing that could have happened to me,' the shepherd said. 'I take great care to ensure that no one does my wolves any harm.'

That is true cooperation, which works as long as wolves stay in one place. If they migrate, or if one of their pack leaders is killed, the situation can quickly change. Let us never forget that wolves are a highly intelligent and very adaptable species. The times when we could comfortably sit back are past. We have to adapt, just as the wolves adapt to us, and to do that we have to be just a step ahead.

And opinions about wolves are changing slowly. Living with wolves is something that the southern European countries have ahead of us. People in Bulgaria, Romania, Italy and Spain have lived with the predators for a long time, and – as opposed to the German love of drama – have done so in a perfectly relaxed fashion. If a wolf kills a sheep, the owners are understandably furious, but they don't immediately demand a cap on the grey robbers.

Kenny Kenner talks about a conversation he had with a Romanian shepherd. When Kenny asked him what he would do if a wolf killed one of his sheep, the shepherd said, 'I'd be ashamed of myself.'

Kenny probed him. 'What do you mean, you'd be ashamed?' He was touched and affected by the answer.

'I'd be ashamed in front of the other shepherds, because it would mean I wasn't a good herdsman. I'm responsible for the animals, and must make sure that nothing happens to them.'

I wish German livestock breeders had this attitude. Shepherds don't need to love the wolves, but they should love their sheep enough to protect them against wolves. That's living wolf-protection. Not all the eternal wailing and complaining, not shifting responsibility to the state, not blaming a predator that is only getting on with its life. But responsibility and an acceptance of the fact that this is how life is, and that wolves are part of that life.

Anyone setting out to educate about wolves in Germany needs strong nerves – and a decent sense of humour, because as with other polarizing subjects (example: refugees) the craziest claims are made.

For several years, for example, the conspiracy theory of the 'car-boot wolves' has regularly appeared on the internet.

These sheep and goats are well protected by an electric
fence. The wolf walks past them

According to this view, wolves are carted from eastern Europe
to the west on lorries and then abandoned. Or else wolf hybrids
are bred in the east and taken illegally across the border to Germany. Hence German wolves are not 'real' wolves and are
therefore not protected. All of these theories have been contradicted by scientific examinations and revealed as fake news.

The fact is that all our wolves migrated naturally to Germany. That also means that we do not have a reintroduction of
wolves, as is often claimed – even by some biologists and wolf
advisers – but a simple remigration. In a reintroduction a threatened animal species that did not previously live in this territory
is brought back by humans. So, for example, in 1995 and 1996
thirty-one timber wolves from Canada were reintroduced to
Yellowstone National Park. However, the first wolves came
back to Germany on their own four paws after the fall of the
Wall.

The media are playing an increasingly important part in
influencing the population. I have been publishing the German

Wolf Magazin since 1991, and in my monthly online newsletter I report on wolves and other wild Canidae. Over the last few years it has been more and more time-consuming for me to separate true and false reports. I see a growing tendency in the media to manipulate public opinion. Every headline containing the word 'wolf' is clearly crying out for attention, and for urgently needed readers. There is little examination, little research, almost nothing but speculation and manipulation. 'Wolf pack outside Hamburg' was one headline. Others leave everything open: 'Twenty sheep killed. Was it a wolf?'

All too often these supposed 'wolves' turn out to be feral dogs. For a layman the difference between a wolf and, for example, a Czechoslovakian wolfdog is barely discernible.

As usual social media joins noisily in. Anyone hoping to find concrete information about wolves will often end up in networks from which we can expect anything but neutrality.

So my advice is, if you are looking for information about wolves, where they live, what they are doing or have done, compare reports carefully, don't believe every so-called 'expert', and regard media contributions by special-interest groups with scepticism. One good source of information is always to be found in the press pages of the environmental offices of the individual regions where wolves have made their homes. Here you will only find confirmed wolf reports.

On our wolf weekend in the Göhrde we also talked to other tourists who were holidaying there because of the peace, the natural environment and also a fascination with wolves. The wolf as a tourist draw is one of the advantages of life with the predator. Where settled packs have been established, and where occasional sightings of wolves are reported, the groupies will never be far away. They create an increase in prosperity in some formerly isolated regions. People come from all parts of the country and even from abroad to see or hear a wild wolf, or at least to take home a few wolf T-shirts and wolf cups. They stay in holiday homes named 'Little Red Riding Hood', order the 'wolf banquet menu' and buy 'wolf's blood' schnapps in the souvenir shops. People have adjusted to the Canidae.

In their climate-neutral organic BioHotel Kenners LandLust, Kenny and Barbara Kenner offer wolf weeks for families with children several times a year. In 2014 the wolf week even won the coveted Golden Palm for tourism from the magazine *Geo Saison* for their programme 'Who's afraid of the big bad wolf?'

Germany is a wolf country again – and it will remain so. The population at large seems to be slowly learning to live with the controversial quadrupeds. Experience has shown that even after twenty years of life with wolves not a single Little Red Riding Hood has been eaten. In a survey by NABU in September 2015 the vote was broadly in favour of wolves. Every second person associated wolves with positive feelings.

Such surveys don't record people who either have a neutral attitude or who are unsettled. They find wolves beautiful and would like to hear a wolf howling, but they would be uncertain if they met one alone in the forest. They teach their children how to treat nature respectfully, but at the same time they want to keep them from everything connected with it – climbing trees, swimming in unfamiliar rivers, crawling in bushes where dangers might lurk. Many people – willingly or otherwise – will have to deal with wolves. They need education, because our attitude to wolves will in the end be crucial for their survival.

This is because wolves are a growing presence in our lives. They are no longer a symbol of untouched nature and the wilderness. As synanthropes they can live unnoticed in the neighbourhood and stroll through villages at dusk. That isn't unusual. In Upper Lusatia people have lived with wolves for many years. The animals circle the villages or walk among the houses at night and even sometimes during the day. In most of these encounters the wolves haven't even noticed that bipeds are anywhere nearby, and vice versa.

In early summer, when sexually mature young wolves begin to migrate in search of their own territory, human beings and wolves will often encounter one another. That does *not* mean that wolves – as is often claimed – are 'bold, contrary to their nature' and hence 'dangerous'. It simply means that during puberty young wolfish whippersnappers are impelled by curiosity to go off on exploratory expeditions, and may approach cars, houses and the occasional jogger. They learn as human children learn: from experience.

At exactly such moments we humans are called upon to behave responsibly. If at this stage the wolves learn that bipeds are really brilliant, for example because they throw them food, clever young wolves will quickly learn to approach humans more and more often. So it is enormously important *under no circumstances to feed wolves*. That should be the supreme rule when dealing with any wild animal.

As I write this, a video about a young wolf in Lower Saxony is causing a stir: the wolf trots across a field, obviously to cross a road, where a woman is going for a run. She panics and screams at the wolf. The wolf stops uneasily. A tractor driver shouts at the wolf: 'Clear off!' The wolf trots on. In the media this event was treated as a shocking moment in various different ways, from 'wolf approaches runner' to 'wolf pursues runner'. Interest groups immediately issued a 'call for action' because a 'red line had been crossed'. I ask you: what red line? What had happened? Nothing! A young wolf walks over a field, looks curiously at a human being and then walks on. That's all. The hype that followed shows how important it is for us to regain a normal relationship with wolves.

There are clear legal rules as regards 'calls for action' in dealing with wolves, which may be consulted in every wolf-management plan. This particular case certainly isn't among them. As endangered animals wolves fall under the very strict rules of European species protection, and that will not change for a very long time. It's up to us to learn to live with them.

Of course there are always people who are afraid in the presence of wild wolves. Perhaps their fear is irrational, but it's there. As wolf conservationists we must take them seriously and respond to their concerns.*

It's completely OK to be afraid when you meet a wolf. We're all afraid of things that are strange to us. But fear doesn't go away if we pretend it doesn't exist. We must face up to it and sometimes just endure it.

I have a lot of respect for children, who are so much braver in response to the unknown than we adults are. In a talk to a school near Celle I asked the pupils who had ever met a wolf. Two girls hesitantly held their hands up. They had met three wolves in the forest.

I asked, 'Were you afraid?'

Violent nodding.

'And? What did you do?'

'Nothing. We stopped and the wolves walked on.'

Bravo! Those little girls did the right thing. A few days later I got a call from the teacher, telling me how proud the girls were about their wolf sighting.

Children are my hope that prejudices can be broken down. They are open, courageous and prepared to embark on new paths. Instinctively they have a natural relationship with animals, which many of us adults lack.

* In the appendix I give advice on the best course of action if you meet a wolf.

Wolves are no better or worse than the people who are trying to protect them. Many of the conflicts in life with wolves will continue to exist in the future.

A century ago, most of the big predators had disappeared almost all over the world. Thanks to a new environmental awareness and improved efforts at conservation they have returned over the last few years. The rise in numbers of wolves, bears and lynx is one of the greatest successes in nature conservation of the twentieth and twenty-first centuries. I have been carrying out intensive work into the protection of wolves, and believe we have reached a new stage of acceptance. Nowadays we are no longer trying to save the wolf, we are learning to live with them.

Our goal is no longer to protect wolves against extinction, but to integrate them into our landscape, our home. For that we need a variety of pragmatic solutions to real problems where people enter into conflict with wolves. We don't need to try to persuade everyone to love wolves, rather we need to get people to accept their presence as part of our landscape.

We forget too easily that it is *not* our task to control nature. It isn't our job to involve ourselves in the lives of wolves. Our job is to protect them and their way of life.

Change is never easy, and sometimes it is far from beautiful. But if it's too much, and it's too big, we get startled and lash out in self-defence, fear and stress. But don't worry – in the end everyone gets used to change. And perhaps one day we will notice that the wolves in the neighbourhood aren't so bad after all, that they haven't yet eaten any children or dogs, that they stay out of our way. Perhaps we will even forget about them now and again when we're walking in the woods. Or else we'll be grateful because they make us perceive the forest with all our senses, just by existing . . . somewhere out there. Then one day we will wake up and notice that we've got used to them, that we can suddenly live with wolves. We'll discover that we no longer flinch in horror at the word 'wolf', but smile.

Why do we need wolves? Human beings have shaped the landscape through agriculture, forestry, hunting, mining and other forms of development. So why would a man-made landscape want to have wolves? That was the question we started with on our wolf weekend.

The answer is simple: because we want to have them there. Yes, there are a lot of people who don't like wolves, but there are also at least as many who do. It's different living in a country that wolves move through. Wolves, bears and elk have returned to Germany; as a result our country is more natural and healthier than it was for many centuries.

My friends and I didn't see any wolves on our wolf weekend in the Göhrde. But finding their trails and knowing that they were there made us happy. We went home knowing that now, in Germany, a wolf might appear outside our front door at any time.

Epilogue

WWWD

WWJD is the abbreviation for 'What would Jesus do?' Church youth leader Janie Tinklenburg discovered the question in 1989 in a book written in 1896 by Charles Sheldon. The idea is to ask, in everything one does, how Jesus Christ would react, act or think in that situation. The slogan, which was embroidered on to friendship bracelets, spread quickly among young American Christians. The bracelets later became a fashion phenomenon. According to Tinklenburg, over 52 million have been sold so far.

Yes, you're still in the right book, and, no, I'm not trying to convert you. On 15 April 2010 I was sitting on my packed suitcases, ready to fly to Yellowstone the next day. It was whelping time. For sixteen years I had always been there in April when the first pups, whose conception I had witnessed in January and February, crawled out of their natal dens. It was always a special event for me, and I looked forward to it.

Then I learned from the television that all flights to and from Europe had been cancelled for the next few days. The Icelandic volcano Eyjafjallajökull had erupted, and air traffic in large parts of northern and central Europe had been halted.

In Yellowstone I had been sitting for decades on one of the biggest supervolcanoes on the planet, and every time I travelled concerned relatives would ask me, 'What would you do if a bear/wolf/puma attacked you?' and 'What if the Yellowstone volcano erupts?' And now a tiny pipsqueak with an unpronounceable name in Iceland had gone off and everything had ground to a standstill. Mother Nature has a unique way of teaching us humility.

But back to WWJD. When I was observing the chaos and still hoped for an opportunity to fly, I remembered that slogan, and on the spur of the moment I decided to repurpose it into WWWD: 'What would wolves do?'

What would wolves do in that situation? Through my years of wolf-watching I have learned what great teachers wolves are, and what masters of adaptation.

Didn't catch the elk when out hunting? OK, let's have a sleep and then give it another go.

Your hunting ground's occupied by a different, larger pack after an outing? It isn't worth risking your life; let's look for another territory or wait till the rivals have gone.

The snow is too deep and wet to get anywhere? Let's use the road and save energy.

No wailing or whingeing or paw-stamping. A situation can't be changed – let's make the best of it or choose an alternative.

Wolves can adapt to any situation. So what would wolves do if they were halted by a volcano? Nothing at all. If waiting is pointless and there's no other way, they'll devote themselves to a different task. I decided to apply what I'd learned from them. Instead of going on waiting for the ash cloud to disperse, I cancelled my flight and wrote an article about the experience.

WWWD has by now become a kind of 'how-to guide' for me. If I find myself stuck in a situation, I ask myself what wolves would do. Their solutions to problems are captivatingly simple.

And yet I can't really *know* what a wolf would do in my situation. I can only draw conclusions from my perspective as a human being and my years of observation in the field.

Wolves are similar to us in many respects. Like them, we are living creatures with a personality, a soul, intelligence and emotions. And yet they couldn't be further removed from us than creatures from another planet.

Sometimes I wonder what it's like to be a wolf. But the more I try to enter their world, thoughts and feelings, the more I recognize with humility that I will never really understand wolves. I'm a human being, and the wolf is a wolf.

Wolves can't be judged according to human standards. They move perfectly in a world that is older and more mature than ours, they have sensory functions that we lost long ago or never developed, and can trust in voices that we will never hear. And yet they are entangled with us, fellow creatures on this wonderful earth of ours.

In Yellowstone I was lucky enough to spend many years observing wolves loving, living and dying. They have taught me how important family is, to show affection to those we love, and to celebrate life even if only for a brief moment in the green grass of Lamar Valley. They have shown me what it means to be a human being.

Words of wolf wisdom:
Love your family,
and look after those entrusted to you.
Never give up.
Never stop playing.

Appendix

Tips for Wolf Tours in Yellowstone and Germany

Maybe after reading this book you will want to observe wild wolves yourself. Without a doubt Yellowstone is the best place in the world to do that. That's why I'd like to give you some tips for wolf trips to Yellowstone National Park. I can also tell you where you might have a chance of seeing a wild wolf in Germany.

Yellowstone

Seasons

The best time for wolf-watching is in winter and spring. In winter (January and February) the big wapiti herds assemble in Lamar Valley. The wolves show themselves in their finest fur coats, and during the mating season one courting wolf or another will forget about the presence of tourists.

The disadvantage: it can get very cold, minus 20 to minus 40 degrees. However, in winter there are significantly fewer tourists around.

In spring (April and May), it is warmer, everything blossoms, a lot of predators have young, and wolf pups come into the world as well. Wolf families now always stay near the natal dens. That means that there are fixed locations for observation. As the wolves have to go hunting a lot now to feed their growing families, the chances of observing a wolf hunt are excellent.

I can't recommend the summer. Many predators withdraw to

higher ground, followed by the wolves. And there are also a lot of tourists in the park. Wolf-watching in late autumn is much better. There is a lot of hunting activity. The young wolves are almost as big as the adults, but they are not yet experienced in hunting. So a wolf pack has to feed many mouths, plus teach the kids to become good hunters. The first night frosts and the spectacular colour of the trees also make this season a visual delight.

Arrival

For wolf watching in winter, only the northern part of Yellowstone is open to motor traffic. There are two airports as starting points: Bozeman and Billings, both in Montana. You will then need to continue in hire cars (four-wheel drive).

In summer, the nearest airports are still Bozeman and Billings, as well as Cody and Jackson in Wyoming. Alternatively, you can also fly to Denver, Salt Lake City or Idaho Falls, and carry on to Yellowstone by car or campervan.

Accommodation

For the 4 million tourists who visit the park annually, there are many hotels in and around the national park. The hotels inside the park are in particularly beautiful spots. It is worth staying here, although you have to book very early, often as much as a year in advance. I recommend direct booking via the website of the park concessionary: www.xanterra.com.

In winter, Gardiner, at the northern entrance to the park, should be your starting point, or else you can book into the Mammoth Hot Springs Hotel in the park.

There are twelve campsites in Yellowstone, although only the Mammoth Hot Springs Campground is open all year round. Some campsites are in grizzly territory (Fishing Bridge), and tents are not allowed, only closed campervans and recreational vehicles. A few sites can be reserved. But most of them work on a first-come, first-served basis. I therefore recommend joining the queue outside the entrance gate very early in the morning so that you find a site when the first campers leave. The best places in the middle of the wolf territory are Pebble Creek Campground and Slough Creek Campground. You will find a summary of the campsites and opening times here: https://www.nps.gov/yell/planyourvisit/campgrounds.htm.

If you want to go hiking for several days and spend the night in the hinterland, you will need a permit from the national park administration. Essentially, you should never hike alone in bear territory, but in groups of at least four. You are also obliged to take bear spray with you. The spray is a mixture of cayenne pepper and tear gas. You will find it in every sports shop or tourist shop and in Yellowstone (price: about $50 or £35).

Phones

Reception is very limited in the park, and only possible in hotels or tourist centres. After many visitors became irritated by tourists holding loud telephone conversations, some phone masts were taken down.

Where are the wolves?

For wolf-watching, the northernmost part of Yellowstone is the most attractive, and it is comfortably accessible by car in every season. Your best chances of viewing all year round are in the valley of the wolves, Lamar Valley, and in Hayden Valley in the summer.

My tip: get up very early to be there at sunrise. Drive slowly through the valley, stop in the lay-bys, turn off your engine, open your windows and listen to the silence. Scour the landscape with your binoculars. If you see a larger group of people anywhere, looking in one direction with scopes or cameras, then it's worth stopping there. We regular wolf-watchers are happy to share our equipment with you.

Sunset is another good time for observing animals, though if you drive home in the dark you should be very careful. Grazing animals move around the park very often here. In winter in particular the bison use the roads for easy (snowless) travel to migrate into or out of the park. They might be in larger groups. It's a good exercise in patience. If you end up in a bison jam and want to overtake them, bear in mind what a park ranger once recommended to me: drive very slowly and packed closely together, bumper to bumper. As soon as there is a gap of even a few centimetres, bison will force their way through, and then all of a sudden your top speed will be the same as bison speed.

And one more tip: Yellowstone is a Mecca for astronomers. There are no large towns in the vicinity, so the starry sky is unique.

Further attractions

Of course you won't go to Yellowstone without visiting its geothermal attractions. The park is home to 60 per cent of the geysers on Earth, including the most famous of the lot, Old Faithful. There are 10,000 hot springs, and the 2,000 earthquakes every year won't let you forget that Yellowstone stands on an active volcano.

My tip for those short of time

If you don't have much time for your stay and still want to see wolves, I advise you to book a guide for a day or two. A guide will give you a summary of where the wolves stay, and over the few days you have, you'll be able to go around on your own steam. There are a lot of guides who offer their services in the park, just google 'Yellowstone guide'.

I prefer to work with the following two very experienced guides, who I have used myself and who I also recommend a lot:

Nathan Varley from Yellowstone Wolf Tracker (https://www.wolftracker.com/) offers a private wildlife guide service as well as packages.

Carl Swoboda from Safari Yellowstone (http://www.safariyellowstone.com/).

Equipment

In addition to seasonally appropriate clothing, you need a good pair of binoculars and a camera with a telephoto lens or a strong zoom. A scope would be ideal. If that's too expensive for your holiday, you can hire scopes, binoculars and tripods in Gardiner: http://opticsyellowstone.com.

In summer, you also need a good mosquito spray, sunglasses and high-factor sun cream – Lamar Valley is at an altitude of 2,500 metres.

How do I identify a wolf?

Now you've done it and you're in Yellowstone. You're waiting excitedly for your first wolf. And there it is – a coyote. One of the hardest tasks for a layperson is to tell a coyote from a wolf. Even we experts don't always find it easy. Here are a few pointers.

Size. Generally speaking wolves are considerably bigger than coyotes. A wolf's body is more massive, its head more compact. Its legs look long and powerful, particularly in summer, when the fur is shorter. When wolves move, their feet often look gangly, and their legs move relatively slowly. Coyotes' legs move faster and they tiptoe.

The *tail position* provides additional help, but it isn't absolutely reliable as an indicator. A wolf's tail often stands vertically upwards – particularly when they are excited. Pack leaders also usually carry their tails raised in the presence of other family members. Coyotes rarely carry their tails as high as wolves.

Coyotes' *ears* are pointed and stand high over their heads. When coyotes behave submissively, their ears are held almost horizontal and stand out at the side ('aeroplane ears'). The ears of wolves are rounder.

Coyotes have a long, pointed *muzzle*, while the wolf's muzzle is short and strong.

The *fur colour* can also be helpful. Black or white Canidae are wolves. But shadows can be deceptive and make an animal look darker than it is. The light grey of some Yellowstone coyotes looks almost white.

Scats and *paw prints* on the ground can be attributed to the species in question, and indicate where the animal has been. Massive scats tend to be made by wolves. If the diameter of a scat is more than 2.5 centimetres, it probably comes from a wolf. The large paw prints of wolves are easily distinguishable from those of coyotes.

Tracks also help to differentiate between the two. Prints (measured without claws) that are longer than 6 centimetres do not come from coyotes, and prints longer than 12 centimetres do not come from dogs. When a wolf is only two months old, its tracks (even those of small females) are larger than those of the coyote. Large dog tracks resemble those of wolves.

Wolf and coyote can also be distinguished by *stride length*. The average stride length of a wolf is 133 centimetres and thus distinctly longer than that of a coyote, which is 60 centimetres.

What to do if a wolf approaches

The Yellowstone wolves know people and (depending on their personality type) are not very afraid of them. If you are lucky enough to be approached by a wild wolf, for all your enthusiasm, please remember to act in the interest of the animal and bear the following in mind:

KEEP YOUR DISTANCE!

Park regulations call for the following distances from animals: 25 metres from a bison, 50 metres from a wolf and 100 metres from a bear. Please keep to these distances. On no account encourage a wolf to approach you. Step backwards and if possible get into your car so that the wolf can continue on their way unimpeded. Don't run away from wolves.

CHASE IT AWAY

In Yellowstone everything that might change animal behaviour is forbidden, and that includes scaring the animals away. If you are standing in a group of wolf-watchers and wolves approach, don't even think about what to do. Stand still with the other visitors and enjoy the view. If you are travelling through the hinterland of the national park and a wolf approaches (and the same applies to an encounter with a wolf in Germany): stand still and make yourself big, clap your hands, address the wolf clearly and chase it away.

DO NOT FEED

A wolf (or coyote or bear or elk or . . . or . . . or . . .) that is fed is a dead wolf. Even if they've only experienced it once, wolves know where and how to get food from humans. The feeding of wild animals, or carelessly leaving food and rubbish lying around at picnic places, is forbidden by law and punished severely.

No dogs

In Yellowstone dogs are only allowed on leads and only on the roads, not in the hinterland. Dogs can attract wolves (and bears). Dogs that are not on leads may be attacked.

Wolf-watching: safety and etiquette

In Yellowstone we have the privilege of observing wild animals in their natural habitat. So that all visitors can enjoy their stay and the animals are disturbed as little as possible, I have drawn up the following ethical rules for my own wolf trips.

- No feeding of wild animals (not even begging squirrels or cheeky ravens).
- Respect closed areas. Signs saying 'No Stopping or walking!' refer to an active den area. They are usually temporary and are there to help the animals raise their young undisturbed. Within such an area you may neither stop your car or drive extremely slowly; it is also forbidden to walk along the road.
- Drive slowly. The top speed permitted is 45 miles an hour. Even that is often too fast, particularly at dusk.
- No howling, yowling, whistling or any other attempts to attract the attention of animals. It disturbs their natural behaviour.
- Respect other visitors to the park. Turn off your engine, speak quietly and close car doors silently. Don't stand in front of other people. Ask permission if you want to use someone else's equipment.
- Don't take anything out of the national park. Removing stones, flowers, antlers or the like is strictly forbidden and can be punished with heavy fines or a jail sentence.

Maps

You will find a map showing the best places for wolf sightings here: http://tinyurl.com/87fyh3b.

A general map of Lamar Valley can be found here: http://www.yellowstone.co/maps/lamarvalley.htm.

The words in purple are the internal names that we wolf-watchers have given to particularly striking locations. You will sometimes hear these names through the radios of a staff member.

You will find general information about Yellowstone National Park and further useful information here: www.nps.gov/yell.

Germany

When I'm in Yellowstone there are very few days when I do *not* see wolves, while in Germany we count ourselves very lucky if we get so much as a hint of a wolf darting past. Our native wolves are extremely retiring – which is good for them.

Federal regions in which packs of wolves have become firmly established are Saxony, Saxony-Anhalt, Brandenburg, Mecklenburg-Vorpommern and Lower Saxony. By now individual wolves passing through can appear almost everywhere in Germany. Most wolves live in former open-cast-mining sites.

There is wolf tourism in Germany too. The focus tends to be less on the observation of wolves than on providing information about them. The organizers of wolf trips inform visitors about wolves and their habitat, they show them tracks, collect scats and might, for example, visit shepherds who work with herd-protecting dogs.

Even if you don't see a wolf, the knowledge that the animals are nearby is a unique experience that is always worthwhile.

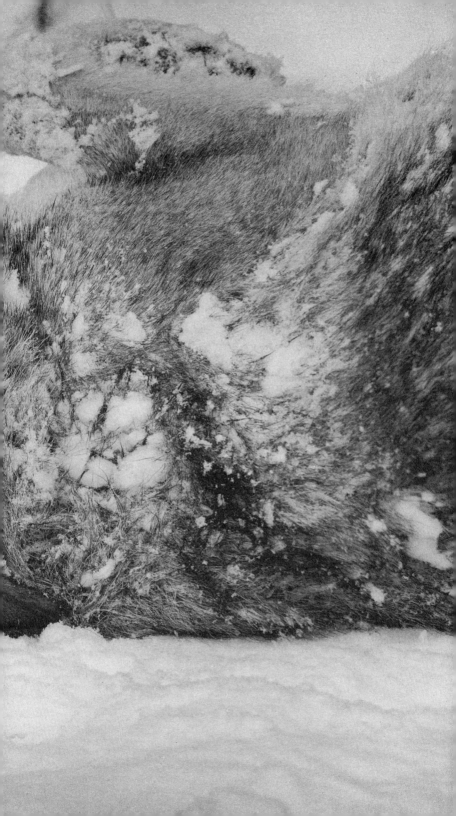

Thanks

Wolves have taught me the importance of family. For that reason I am most grateful to my two- and four-legged family. Without you I couldn't live my dream. Thank you for your love and support.

The fact that this book, so close to my heart, has become a reality is principally thanks to my literary agent Dr Uwe Neumahr from Agence Hoffman in Munich, who believed in me and the project and who always built me back up again when I had succumbed to a creative I'll-never-make-it depression.

Thanks to my editor Jessica Hein for the freedom she gave me with the manuscript, and for her confidence in me.

The Ludwig Verlag team gave me a warm welcome. Thanks for that, and for our terrific collaboration. I would like to thank Maren Wetcke for her sensitive and intelligent copy-edit, which was a great help to me and gave me great pleasure.

Andrea Märtens: your spiritual support and encouragement during the long writing process was an inestimable help to me. Your friendship is a gift.

Peter Wohlleben: you are my 'green alter ego'. Not only do we share the same views about nature and the environment, but at times of doubt and insecurity you gave me helpful advice.

Günther Bloch: as co-authors we have written a number of books together, as field researchers we often exchange information about the behaviour of wolves. With your retirement I will miss our close collaboration.

The wolves of Yellowstone – they have become my second family and an important part of my life. My observations over many years would not have been possible without the help of Rick McIntyre, the 'Wolf Man'. Laurie Lyman, with her daily email reports, makes me feel as if I'm still there. To list all the regular wolfaholics of Yellowstone would stretch the book to bursting point. They have all become good friends.

For many years I have carried out two or three wolf-watching trips every year. The 'groupies' from Germany have sometimes brought me back down to earth with their enthusiasm, and made it clear to me that you *can't* take being surrounded by wolves for granted – as I sometimes feel I'm doing if I spend too much time in wolf country. Particular thanks to my 'Musketier' group – Karin, Andrea and Joe. I've rarely laughed till I cried as I have with you. I hope we'll be able to do it again.

The Zeiss company in Wetzlar sponsors scopes and binoculars for my observations. Without this wonderful equipment some of my field observations wouldn't have been possible.

Last of all, I would like to thank the wolves, who have become a part of my life. May your descendants be numerous in the mountains and valleys of Yellowstone.

Sources

The Importance of Family

Bloch, Günther, and Elli H. Radinger, *Wölfisch für Hundehalter: Von Alpha, Dominanz und anderen populären Irrtümern*, Stuttgart, 2010
https://www.shell.de/ueber-uns/die-shell-jugendstudie/werte-der-jugend.html

Leadership on the Alpha Principle

Sands, Jennifer, 'Social Dominance, Aggression and Faecal Glucocorticoid Levels in a Wild Population of Wolves', *Animal Behaviour*, Volume 67, Issue 3 (March 2004), pp. 387–96

Smith, Doug, Dan Stahler and Debra Guernsey, *Yellowstone Wolf Project*, Annual Report 2004, 2005, 2006, National Park Service, Yellowstone Center for Resources

Zeug, Katrin, '*Süchtig nach Anerkennung*', *Zeit.de*, 11.06.2013, http://www.zeit.de/zeit-wissen/2013/04/psychologie-soziale-anerkennung

The Strength of Women

Estés, Clarissa Pinkola, *Die Wolfsfrau: Die Kraft der weiblichen Urinstinkte*, Munich, 1993

The Wisdom of Old Age

https://www.nps.gov/yell/learn/ys-24-1-territoriality-and-inter-pack-aggression-in-gray-wolves-shaping-a-social-carnivores-life-history.htm

The Art of Communication

https://www.galileo.tv/earth-nature/forscher-entschluesseln-die-wolfs
  sprache
Bloch, Günther, *Gruppenverhalten, Dominanzbeziehungen und Kommuni-kation*, seminar script, May 2008, Hunde-Farm 'Eifel'
http://www.mein-medizinportal.de/themenwelten/alters-und-palliativ
  medizin/die-heilkraft-der-beruehrung_17212902.htm
Suddendorf, Thomas, *The Gap: The Science of What Separates Us from Other Animals*, Basic Books, New York, 2013

The Longing for Home

https://wolf-sachsen. de/de/wolfsmanagement-in-sn/kat-struktur-man
  agement/5-berwolf/katwolf/33-art-biologie-und-lebensweise
https://www.nps.gov/yell/learn/ys-24-1-territoriality-and-inter-pack-aggression-in-gray-wolves-shaping-a-social-carnivores-life-history.htm
Hamilton's Rule: https://en.wikipedia.org/wiki/Kin_selection#
  Hamilton's_rule
http://www.staff.uni-mainz.de/neumeyer/Vergleichende/Altruismus.
  html

I'm Off Then

Bloch, Günther, and Elli H. Radinger, *Der Wolf kehrt zurück: Mensch und Wolf in Koexistenz?*, Stuttgart, 2017, p. 119

Merrill, S. B., and L. D. Mech, 'Details of Extensive Movements by Minnesota Wolves', *American Midland Naturalist* 144 (2000), pp. 428–33

Linnell, J. D. C., et al., 'The Origins of the Southern Scandinavian Wolf *Canis Lupus* Population: Potential for Natural Immigration in Relation to Dispersal Distances, Geography and Baltic Ice', *Wildlife Biology* 11:4 (2005), p. 386

Almost Best Friends

Heinrich, Bernd, 'Teamplayer', *Dogs* 6 (2010), pp. 114–17

Stahler, Daniel, 'Common Ravens, Corvus Corax, Preferentially Associate with Grey Wolves, Canis Lupus, as a Foraging Strategy in Winter', *Animal Behavior* 64 (2002), pp. 283–90

Bloch, Günther, 'Wolf und Rabe: Langzeituntersuchungsergebnisse zur Sozialisation und zum Zusammenleben von zwei Arten', *Wolf Magazin* 2 (2013)

Heinrich, Bernd, *Die Weisheit der Raben: Begegnungen mit den Wolfsvögeln*, Munich, 2002

Bloch, G., and P. Paquet, *Wolf (Canis lupus) & Raven (Corvus corax): the Co-Evolution of 'Team Players' and their Living-together in a Social-Mixed Group*, seminar script, May 2008, Hunde-Farm 'Eifel'

Planning for Success – The Wolf Method

McAllister, Ian and Karen, *The Great Bear Rainforest: Canada's Forgotten Coast*, Pender Harbour, 1997

https://www.ncbi.nlm.nih.gov/pmc/articles/PMC4229308

The Game of Life

Personal conversation with Günther Bloch (German wolf researcher in Canada) about the wolves in Banff National Park

Bekoff, Marc, *The Emotional Lives of Animals*, Novato, 2008

Bloch, Günther, and Elli H. Radinger, *Wölfisch für Hundehalter: Von Alpha, Dominanz und anderen populären Irrtümern*, Stuttgart, 2010

Let's Just Save the World

Berger, K. M., and E. M. Gese, 'Does Interference Competition with Wolves Limit the Distribution and Abundance of Coyotes?', *Journal of Animal Ecology* 76 (2007), pp. 1075–85

Ripple, William J., *Trophic Cascades in Yellowstone: The First 15 Years after Wolf Reintroduction*, https://ir.library.oregonstate.edu/xmlui/bitstream/handle/1957/25603/ RippleWilliam.Forestry.Trophic CascadesYellowstone.pdf

Wolf Medicine

http://www.laweekly.com/film/military-veterans-work-with-rescued-wolves-in-the-documentary-the-war-in-between-8108078

Of Men and Wolves

Balthasar, Cord, *Warum Kugelschreiber tödlicher sind als Blitze: Verblüffende Statistiken über die Gefahren und Risiken unseres Lebens*, Munich, 2014

http://dex1.info/diese-20-tiere-toten-die-meisten-menschen-auf-der-welt-der-1-und-der-letzte-platz-sind-unglaubliche-uberraschungen/
http://www.hna.de/kassel/kreis-kassel/wolf-angst-interview-psycho logen-harald-euler-6393026.html
http://www.spiegel.de/spiegel/print/d-133575645.html

Welcome Wolf

Bloch, Günther, and Elli H. Radinger, *Der Wolf kehrt zurück: Mensch und Wolf in Koexistenz?*, Stuttgart, 2017
https://www.wolf-sachsen.de/en/wolfsmanagement-in-sn/monitoring-und-forschung
http://www.az-online.de/uelzen/stadt-uelzen/wolf-ueberrascht-schaefer-hilft-7445416.html
http://www.az-online.de/uelzen/az-tv/grosser-schock-moment-wolf-naehert-sich-einer-joggerin-7445477.html

Picture Credits

Picture Editing: Tanja Zielezniak

All images are from Koppfoto/Gunther Kopp, Dunzweiler, with the exception of: Askani, Tanja: 46; Cornilsen, Corina: 222/223; Foard, Marlene: 26; Hamann, Michael: 209; Hartman, Dan: 49; Hogston, Gerry: 15; Mauritius-image: 58 (NPS photo/ Alamy/Diane Renkin), 76 (Park Collection/Alamy/Dan Stahler), 98/99, 110/111, 160/161, 179, 188 (NPS Photo/Alamy), 162 (Nature and Science/Alamy), 224 (Raimund Linke), 8/9 (Tom Uhlman/ Alamy); Mark Miller Photos: 39, 44/45, 100; Mayer, Michael: 200, 201, 202, 10, 24; National Park Service, public domain: xii (NPS/Jacob W. Frank), 112 (NPS/Dan Stahler), (NPS); Private Archive Elli H. Radinger: x/xi.